BUSINESS DEVELOPMENT AND ENTREPRENEURSHIP

IN A STRESSFUL ECONOMY

DR. ANTHONY F. CIUFFO

 www.trafford.com
North America & international
toll-free: 1 888 232 4444 (USA & Canada)
fax: 812 355 4082

Dedication and Thank you

This project is dedicated to my wife, Joan my inspiration, my lifelong friend, my one and only love, my everything and to our three children, AnnMarie, Michael, and Anthony, Jr. We are very proud of all of you. Mom and I also want to thank your spouses, Joe, Susan, and Michelle. Thank you for marrying our children and supporting our family motto:

"Hard Work Pays Off"

Contents

Tables

Figures

Appendices

Appendix 1

Appendix 2

Appendix 3

Preface

Many of us have experienced the worst economic conditions of our lifetimes. The good news is that I am confident that this, too, will pass. The bad news is that things could get worse before they get better. It is difficult to determine if this problem will disappear quickly; however, rest assured that bad economic cycles do end. The economy moves in cycles, and sooner or later tough times will become good times, which will eventually become bad times once again. How long each cycle will last is difficult to determine; it depends on the economic actions taken by political administrations. Months before a turnaround starts to manifest itself, there will be signs that those with sharp eyes will be able to detect. It is worth paying attention to these signs and being aware that the recession is starting to turn around. Keep an eye on statistics addressing unemployment rate, housing development, financial market trends, spending, retail sales, construction, and manufacturing. These are all barometers that take the pulse of the economy and indicate how far along the road to recovery the economy is.

Planning, information, and knowledge are the tickets to recovery and survival. A lack of planning, information, and knowledge is a recipe for disaster.

This book will examine how principles of economics, entrepreneurship, and business contribute to operating a growing, successful business. It is not the intent of this project to address how to start or operate a successful business; rather, this project seeks to identify and determine the elements that produce survival, growth, and success.

Additionally, it is necessary to determine what constitutes success and if success for one businessperson means the same for another businessperson. This research journal attempts to identity and establish what success really means.

The objective is also to address the characteristics and attributes of a successful entrepreneur and what role they play in the successful operation of a business. In addition, this study will address the various elements of developing a successful business, as well as how to help both new and existing businesses survive.

Establishing a competency in entrepreneurship and business development will enhance a prospective entrepreneur's chances of survival. It is the intent of this project to conduct an intense literature review to ascertain the type of information available concerning all aspects of entrepreneurship and business that are necessary in developing a successful business.

In an effort to enhance the learning process, each chapter will begin by outlining the learning objectives and conclude with an explanation of the key terms mentioned in the chapter.

Introduction

There exist today a number of publications, journals, and articles that give advice on how to start your own business or operate a successful enterprise. This journal is not one of them. The focus or mission statement of this publication is to identify and determine, through research, the elements that constitute establishing, maintaining, and developing a successful business operation in a depressed economic situation.

To succeed we must diligently watch the messages and signs our weakened economy is trying to relate to us. Such signs as unemployment insurance claims, length of time houses are on the market, automobile sales, banks' mortgage activities, mortgages, and the number of people flying at major airports all indicate whether consumers are starting to gain confidence in the nation's economy. Recognizing these indicators requires diligence and knowledge.

To stack the odds in their favor, entrepreneurs must gain essential knowledge, concepts, and tools prior to and while taking the start-up plunge. This thirst for knowledge sparked a significant call for researching the entrepreneurial process and the elements that constitute business success and growth. Never in the history of business schools has there been such a demand from students for entrepreneurship education, a demand that Bygrave tells us has not been meet satisfactorily (1997, p. xiv).

Much of what was known previously has been reinforced and refined, and there is also an avalanche of new insights concerning entrepreneurship.

A review of recent research on entrepreneurship shows that most of the research concerns entrepreneurship in countries other than the United States (Mador, 2000). This may be because businesses in America have always involved a kind of entrepreneurship that businesses in other countries have not. This is truly a sign that the entrepreneurial revolution has gone global. Yet as Americans we can learn from all sources, domestic and international, and derive many benefits from those entrepreneurs who pursue risk-filled but successful efforts and find change and opportunities. Common sense dictates that there is no substitute for the real thing: starting your own business. However, short of this, it is possible for future entrepreneurs to gain exposure to the elements that go into making a successful enterprise grow and prosper.

Core curriculum elements of knowledge include as the following subjects:

- Obtaining supply and creating demand

- Entrepreneurship as the fulfilling of consumer needs

- The invention process

- Knowledge of patents, copyrights, and trademarks

- Cost/benefit analysis

- Business ethics

- Location selection

- Record keeping

- The present and future value of money

- Business communication with an emphasis on concise memo writing, internet based communications, such as E-Mail, and speaking on the phone

- Debt versus equity financing

- Venture capital

- Balance sheets and income statements

- Franchising

- Advantages and disadvantages of sole proprietorships, partnerships, and corporations

- The production/distribution chain

- How to register a business

- Time management and goal setting

- Quality and customer service

- Negotiation strategies

- Advertising and marketing along with the basics of selling

The core elements of knowledge listed above shall be considered, for the purpose of this journal, internal elements of success (the elements over which an entrepreneur has direct control). All other elements will be considered external elements (the elements over which an entrepreneur does not have control but which he or she can adopt to survive in a given environment). Each chapter will be identified as "Internal" or "External."

We have entered into the entrepreneurial age. We are now involved with an entrepreneurial revolution that is transforming and renewing economies worldwide (Bygrave, 1999). With a global marketplace now a reality, entrepreneurs and small businesses are seizing opportunities at a rate never before equaled.

New business opportunities spring up daily, offering tremendous potential to those with the ability to see them, the desire to reach for them, and the tenacity to capture them. A good eye, a strong heart, and a tenacious temperament do not guarantee success in this whirlwind of competition. To succeed, an entrepreneur also needs a very precious commodity: knowledge. There are endless opportunities for those with entrepreneurial zeal. However, the fact is that a single entrepreneur will be able to launch and build only a few good businesses, probably no more than three or four during his or her energetic and productive years (Timmons & Olin, 1999, p. 1).

In essence, entrepreneurship is what America does best. Entrepreneurs founded the United States, building the country by creating small businesses, farms, ranches, and mines. During the Industrial Revolution and after World War II, people began worshiping the prospect of going into business, craving independence and job security. These goals could be achieved through big business, big farms, big ranches, big mines, and big city and federal jobs (Price, 1999, p. xiii).

Today, we are surrounded by economic evidence that entrepreneurship is truly the trend of the twenty-first century. In today's economy, size is no longer the quintessential goal for businesses. In fact, size, once considered an essential ingredient for success, is becoming a liability for many companies (Price, 1999, p. xiii).

In the United States, entrepreneurial companies created the personal computer, biotechnology, fast food, and overnight package delivery industries; transformed the retailing industry; revitalized the steel industry; and invented the integrated circuit and the microprocessor. Every sector of the economy feels the influence of entrepreneurs (Bygrave, 1997, p. 1).

Price (1999) points out that new business start-ups dominate our economic growth at the rate of more than seven hundred thousand start-ups per year, double the rate of a decade ago and eight times what it was in the 1950s at the height of the industrial period.

Information provided by the U S Small Business Administration office shows that small businesses provided virtually all the new jobs that became available from 1991 to 1995 and comprised 99.7 percent of all employers in 1993. According to the *Small Business Advocate,* today one of every three households includes someone who has had a primary role in a new or emerging business. The latest statistics report that 1.1 to 1.2 million new American businesses are created annually.

Research sponsored by the National Federation of Independent Business estimates that the annual number of new start-ups is closer to 3.5 million. This number does not include what is called the "underground business economy" (uncounted part-time and full-time home-based businesses). Research declares that on average, firms with fewer than one hundred employees create the majority of new jobs in the U.S. economy (Price, 1999, p. xiv).

Entrepreneurs are changing the way we live, work, think, and learn. Many are jumping on this exciting entrepreneurial wave. It has been proven that visions of owning your own business and being your own boss can become reality with proper research, information planning, and entrepreneurial training.

Many opportunities have emerged for women entrepreneurs and minorities. Ebert and Griffin (2000, p. 157) cite the following statistics:

- The number of **black-owned** businesses has increased by 46 percent during the most recent five-year period; current data puts the number at about 621,000. Black purchasing power topped $530 billion in 1999, up from just over $300 billion in 1990. This increase of 73 percent far outstrips the 57 percent increase experienced by all Americans.

- The number of **Hispanic-owned** businesses has grown at an even faster rate, 76 percent, and is now about 862,000.

- **Other ethnic groups** are making their presence felt among U.S. business owners. For instance, business ownership among Asian and Pacific Islanders has increased 56 percent to over 600,000. Although the number of businesses owned by American Indians and Alaska Natives is still somewhat small at slightly over 100,000, this total nevertheless represents a five-year increase of 93 percent.

- The number of **women entrepreneurs** is also growing rapidly, and women-owned businesses are the largest emerging segment of the small-business market. Women-owned businesses are an economic force that no bank or financial institution can afford to overlook.

- Entrepreneurial opportunities also exist for the **physically disabled,** many of whom are discovering that the only way they can do the work they enjoy is by starting a business that accommodates their disability (Price, 1999, p. 2).

This project will focus on identifying the necessary ingredients for business development. For the purpose of this study, each element of success will be classified as internal or external. An internal element, such as knowledge and attributes, can be affected and changed individually by the entrepreneur. An external element cannot be changed or affected so easily by the businessperson. Elements like the economy, the economic cycle, the barriers of entry, and "luck" will be considered external elements. This journal will review elements including:

- The economy and the American business system

- Understanding how the economic cycle will affect the business enterprise

- Understanding entrepreneurship and the small business

- Attributes and characteristics of an entrepreneur

- Obtaining the necessary knowledge for success

- What exactly is success?

- Trends and challenges

- The management process

- Organizational structure

- The marketing process and human behavior

Each chapter will explore different elements pertaining to the success of an Entrepreneur and his or her business venture.

Chapter 1 will explore:

- The U.S. economic system

- The importance of studying economic theory

- The law of supply and demand

- Competition

- Monopoly

- Employment

Chapter 2 will explore:

- Business cycles

- Inflation

- Recession

- Depression

- Recovery

- Cyclical impact of the business cycle

- Unemployment

- Full employment

  Chapter 3 will explore:

- The importance a family plays in the success of a business

- The importance of self-evaluation

- What success is all about

  Chapter 4 will explore:

- What goes into a self-evaluation

- An actual self-evaluation test

- How to determine if you are entrepreneur material

  Chapter 5 will explore:

- How individuals develop their code of ethics

- The consequences of unethical practices

- Why ethics are important to businesses and in the workplace

- How ethics and social responsibility apply to customers, employees, and investors.

  Chapter 6 will explore

- The importance of advance planning

- Understanding the importance of threshold decision making

- Understanding the importance of marketing

- Other internal elements for survival and growth

- Financing business ventures and growth

Chapter 7 will explore:

- Strategies for success and growth

- Aspects of the Federal Governments Small Business Administration (SBA)

- Developing a vision for the business

- Benefits of total immersion into the business

- Best practices of successful businesses for weathering an economic recession

Chapter 1

The American Economic System: External Element

Learning Objectives:

- To identify and describe the different types of economic systems

- To define and describe the nature of the American business system

- To learn how the American economic system affects the success and failure of American businesses

- To relate supply and demand to the success and failure of enterprises

- To understand the various degrees of competition in the U.S. economic system

- To understand how competition relates to the success and failure of American enterprises

- To understand the criteria for evaluating the success of an economic system and its business enterprises

- To understand how the federal government attempts to manage the U.S. economy

Why Study Economic Theory?

Small business owners are usually extremely involved with their business's operation, which means they have little or no time to worry about economic theory. What entrepreneurs rely on is hands-on action, concrete experience, and no-nonsense advice from people who have been there and back. However, entrepreneurs recognize that economic theory can and will affect their business enterprise. For this reason, it behooves an entrepreneur to step back and take a break from the mechanics of starting and operating a business and consider the big picture: the economic concepts that will make

or break a business venture. For example, Jack A. Ablin, CFA, senior vice president, and

chief investment officer of Harris Bank, clearly reflects on the elements affecting the

economy. On Harrisdirect.com, he states that:

> Today's economy is like a vehicle fueled by four distinct but highly
> combustible elements: aggressive monetary policy, tax givebacks, heady
> government spending and a weak dollar. Together they are powering an
> expansion that is moderate, but healthy.
> Much of the recent economic growth is the result of increased business
> spending on equipment, software and commercial construction. Business
> investment rose at an annualized rate of 9.3 percent in the last quarter of 2003, a
> clear reflection that confidence among business leaders is raising after three years
> of cost trimming and light purse-strings. Residential construction also contributed
> mightily to economic growth. Despite the good news, a weak job market
> continues to cloud the economic outlook. (March 2004)

By understanding the fundamentals of macroeconomic forces that make the

world's modern market economies run, entrepreneurs can ensure that their business

enterprises will be successfully woven into the economic system. Failure to understand

the importance of rudimental theories of economics, such as those mentioned by Ablin,

will surely spell disaster for new businesses.

Experience indicates that many entrepreneurs are not cognizant of the

impact the national economy has on the survival and growth of their business enterprises.

Although many are aware of the impact of supply and demand, few truly realize the

importance of "market economics."

Supply and demand are the two principal economic forces that drive an open market. The function of any marketplace is to provide a setting in which supply and demand can operate to establish price (Bangs & Pinson, 1999, p. 22).

Having knowledge of the laws of supply and demand will help entrepreneurs make sound business decisions. If an entrepreneur thinks the demand for a product is going to rise, it would be wise to start selling that product, because the price that people are willing to pay for is going to rise. For example, the price of heating oil generally rises in the winter because the demand for heating oil in certain areas rises as well depending on the severity of the winter weather. Naturally, as demand dissipates, prices also decrease—thus the law of supply and demand.

It is important for entrepreneurs to note that the laws of supply and demand work best in competitive markets. When businesses are competing with one another, they try to attract consumers by lowering prices, improving quality, and developing new products and services (Mariotti, 2000, p. 69)

Government regulations, or anything else that keeps entrepreneurs from entering a market, will make the market less competitive. Less competition leads to higher prices, poorer quality, and fewer new products and services (Mariotti, 2000, p. 69).

In the marketplace, the idea of supply and demand determines how prices for goods and services are set. Essentially, when supply increases and demand remains stable, prices go down; when demand increases and supply remains stable, prices go up. Greater demand means producers can raise their prices because eager consumers will compete for the product (Bangs & Pinson, 1999, p. 22).

According to Ebert and Griffin, a market is a mechanism for exchange between the buyers and sellers of a particular good or service (2000, p. 10). To better understand how a market economy works, think of how a retailer purchases products. If you are shopping for a container of milk and one retailer is selling it for $1.00 per gallon and the other is selling the same milk for $1.50, the customer is apt to purchase it from the store selling it for $1.00 per gallon. However, if the $1.00-per-gallon milk is outdated, the customer may choose the $1.50-per-gallon milk. In essence, both the buyer and the seller have the freedom to decide how much to charge and what to buy. The businessperson must be aware of what motivates the customer to buy a product and what price a customer is willing to pay for that product.

Types of Economic Systems

Often, the employment status and income level of the buying public is a powerful force in consumers' decisions of whether to buy and how much to spend. When job opportunities are scarce or wage levels low, demand usually drops. Thousands of markets for goods and services might be affected drastically by a single major employer.

It is important for an entrepreneur or other businessperson to become familiar with the economic system that determines the success or failure of his or her enterprise.

Understanding the complex nature of the U.S. economic system is essential to understanding the environment in which U.S. businesses operate. Specifically, examining markets, the nature of Supply and Demand private enterprise, and degrees of competition is critical, since all of these are necessary ingredients for operating a successful enterprise.

An economic system is a nation's system of allocating its resources (Ebert & Griffin, 2000, p. 8). Different types of economic systems manage the factors of production in different ways. Some systems have ownership as a private transaction. In other systems, the federal government owns production. Several major economic systems exist today:

Planned economy: A planned economy relies on a centralized government to control all or most factors of production and to make all or most production and allocation decisions. The two most basic forms of planned economies are communism and socialism.

According to German economist Karl Marx, communism is a system in which the government owns and operates all sources of production. Marx envisioned a society in which individuals contributed according to their abilities and received economic benefits according to their needs. Marx also expected that government ownership of production factors would be temporary and that eventually the workers would gain ownership. This economic and political system was embraced by communist systems in the Soviet Union. In the early 1990s, it was renounced by most communist countries as a political and economic system. They began to lean toward a free-enterprise system, such as capitalism (Ebert & Griffin, 2000, p. 10).

In plain terms, communism aims to equalize social conditions; specifically, it strives to abolish inequalities in the possession of property by distributing all wealth equally to all or by holding all wealth in common for the equal use and advantage of all. The way of achieving this goal is by the collectivization of all private property. In essence, communism requires that no individual may own anything exclusively and privately: not the product of his or her work (or of his or her mind) or any personal material benefit he or she may achieve. Freedom of expression tends to be mediated by the state for the same reason: to maintain the integrity of the masses. In essence, communism is a welfare state and runs counter to the capitalistic system of free enterprise and wealth building. It seems that communism's final chapters were written in the early 1990s, with its collapse in the Soviet Union.

Socialism: Socialism is a partially planned system in which the government owns and operates selected major industries. In such mixed economies, the government may control banking, communication, transportation, and industries that produce such basic goods as oil and steel. Smaller businesses, such as clothing stores and restaurants, are privately owned. Countries like France allow free-market operations in most economic areas but maintain government control in others, such as healthcare. Government planners in Japan give special centrally planned assistance to new industries that are expected to grow (Ebert & Griffin, 2000, p. 12).

Socialism shares the same collective view as communism. Its means of production, distribution, and exchange are mostly but not entirely owned by the state and used, at least in theory, on behalf of the people whose need is decided by the legislator. The ideal behind socialism is that the capitalist system is intrinsically unfair because it concentrates wealth in a few hands and does nothing to safeguard the overall welfare of the majority. However, this has proven to be a fallacy (Political Systems Explained, 2004, p. 4). Because all property must be created before it is distributed, modern socialists allow some free-market enterprise to exist in order to feed off its production. This fact seems to admit that the free market is the best way to produce wealth.

Under socialism, the state redistributes the wealth of society in a more equitable way, according to the judgment of the legislator. Socialism as a system is anathema to most Americans, but it is accepted in Europe. Socialism is a system of expropriation of private property in order to distribute it to various groups considered by the legislator to warrant it, usually the unemployed, ill, young, old, and those with political pull.

Capitalism: People have many different ideas about what capitalism means. Capitalism is not a system of force imposed by people; rather, it is a lack of such a system. It is what happens when people are free from the force of other people. In order to have people who are free of the force of natural conditions, something must be done to make those conditions better for mankind. This is exactly what people have been doing by inventing the wheel, producing energy, and engaging in all that followed. These advancements are products of people's minds, initiative, and creativity.

Unlike communism and socialism, capitalism does not aim at equalization because people are free to choose their own paths. Some people have more opportunities (but not more freedom), but that in no way gives anyone the right to rob them of their possessions and give them to someone else. The demise of communism can be attributed to a lack of motivation of the workforce. Capitalism is clearly a market economy paradigm.

Market economies are based on principles of markets, not governments, which determine what, when, and where to produce. Capitalism provides for private ownership and encourages entrepreneurship by offering profits as an incentive. Businesses can provide whatever goods and services they want and charge whatever prices they choose. Similarly, customers can choose how and where to spend their money (Ebert & Griffin, 2000, pp. 9–10).

Contrary to popular belief, capitalism is not a system as such. Instead, it is the consequence of individual liberty and corresponding rights (the right to own that which you create or are born owning). Under the capitalistic system, anyone can work hard and receive the benefits of private enterprise, unlike the social and communistic systems.

See **Table 1** for a comparison of the three economic and political systems.

Table 1: A Comparison of Capitalism, Socialism, and Communism

<u>**Capitalism**</u>	<u>**Socialism**</u>	<u>**Communism**</u>
Policy of the West	Policy of the East	Policy of the East
Elections	Autocratic/Dictatorship	Dictatorship
Free-market enterprise	Possibly used for need of all	Surrendered for the needs of all
Workers and businesses enjoy the rewards of their hard work	Certain industries impose the hard work of some for the needs of all	All enjoy the rewards of the hard work of one
Freedom of religion and government	Some religious freedom, some free elections	No religious freedom or free elections
People free to conduct their own lives	No freedoms	No freedoms
Advocates that hard work pays off	Most industries belong to the state	Advocates that no individual may own anything exclusively

The Laws of Supply and Demand

On all economic levels, the forces of supply and demand determine decisions about what to buy and what to sell. Demand is the willingness and ability of buyers to purchase a product, good, or service. Supply is the willingness and ability of producers to offer a good or service for sale. Knowledge and understanding of the concepts of supply and demand will help a business enterprise achieve a steady course of growth potential. Generally speaking, Ebert and Griffin (2000, p. 13) describe the supply and demand laws as follows:

- **Law of demand:** Principle that buyers will purchase more of a product as its price drops and less as its price increases.

- **Law of supply:** Principle that producers will offer more of a product for sale as its price rises and less as its price drops.

- **Demand and supply schedule:** Assessment of the relationships between different levels of demand and supply at different price levels. See **Table 2** for an example.

- **Supply Curve:** Graph showing how many units of a product will be supplied (offered for sale) at different prices. See **Figure 1**.

- **Demand Curve:** Graph showing how many units of a product will be supplied (offered for sale) at different prices. See **Figure 2**.

- **Market Price (or Equilibrium Price):** Profit-maximizing price at which the quantity of goods demanded and the quantity of goods supplied are equal. See **Figure 3**.

- **Surplus:** Situation in which quantity supplied exceeds quantity demanded.

- **Shortages:** Situation in which quantity demanded exceeds quantity supplied.

Please note that an explanation of **Figure 1, Figure 2,** and **Figure 3** will be provided after the graphs.

Table 2: Demand and Supply Schedules: Source: Ebert & Griffin, 2000, p. 14

Price	Quantity of Product Demanded	Quantity of Product Supplied
$2.00	2000	100
$4.00	1900	400
$6.00	1600	600
$8.00	1200	800
$10.00	1000	1000
$12.00	800	1200
$14.00	600	1300
$16.00	400	1600
$18.00	200	1800
$20.00	100	2000

Supply Curve

Figure 1: Supply Curve: Source: Ebert & Griffin, 2000, p. 14

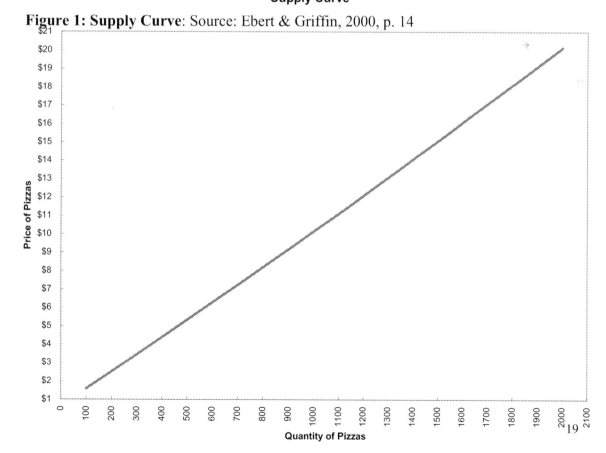

Figure 2: Demand Curve- Source: Ebert & Griffin (2000, p. 14)

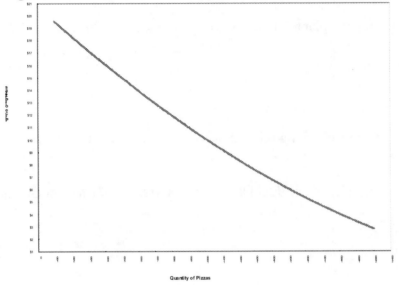

Quantity of Pizzas

Figure 3: Supply & Demand Source: Ebert & Griffin, 2000, p. 14

Equilibrium Price (Demand and Supply)

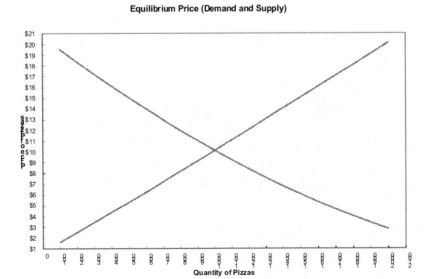

Quantity of Pizzas

Explanation of Figure 1, Figure 2, and Figure 3

Figure 1, Supply Curve: When the price is low, more people are willing to buy the product. Manufacturers, however, do not have the money to invest in making the product and so make fewer. Supply, therefore, is limited. Only when the price goes up will the manufacturers be willing and able to increase supply (Ebert & Griffin, 2000, p. 14).

Figure 2, Demand Curve: When the price is high, fewer people are willing to pay for it. But when the price goes down, more people are willing to buy the product. At the lower price, in other words, more people "demand" the product (Ebert & Griffin, 2000, p. 14).

Figure 3: Supply & Demand (Equilibrium Price): When manufacturers increase supply in order to satisfy demand, there will ultimately be a point at which the price that they can earn is the same as the price that a maximum number of customers are willing to pay. That point is the market price, or equilibrium price (Ebert & Griffin, 2000, p. 14).

It is important for entrepreneurs and businesspeople to be aware of the principles of supply and demand in order to understand what compels customers to buy products.

Degrees of Competition

McConnell & Brue (2001, pp 438-439) indicates that competition and knowledge of the levels of competition can and will determine the success or failure of a business enterprise. Not all industries are equally competitive. Economists have identified four basic degrees of competition within a private enterprise:

1. In **pure competition**, a very large number of firms produce a standardized product (for example, wheat or peanuts). New firms can enter the industry very easily.

2. At the other extreme, a **pure monopoly** is a market in which one firm is the sole seller of a product or service (for example, a local electric company). The entry of additional firms is blocked so that the firm is the industry. Because there is only one product, there is no product differentiation.

3. **Monopolistic competition** is characterized by a relatively large number of sellers producing differentiated products (for example, women's clothing, furniture, or books). Differentiation is the basis for product promotion and development. Entry into a monopolistically competitive industry is quite easy.

4. Finally, in an **oligopoly**, there are just a few sellers, which is interpreted that pricing and output decisions are interdependent. Each firm is affected by the decisions of rivals and must take these decisions into account when determining its own price-output behavior. Products may be standardized (steel or aluminum) or differentiated (automobiles and computers). Generally, entry into oligopolistic industries is very difficult.

Table 3 below summarizes the four types of competition.

Table 3: Degrees of Competition

Source: McConnell & Brue, 2001, p. 439

Characteristic	Pure Competition	Monopolistic Competition	Oligopoly	Pure Monopoly
Number of firms	Large number	Many	Few	One
Type of product	Standardized	Differentiated	Standardized or differentiated	Unique; no close substitutes
Control over price	None	Some, within limits	Considerable with collusion	Considerable
Conditions of entry	Very easy, no obstacles	Relatively easy	Significant obstacles present	Blocked
Nonprice competition	None	Considerable emphasis on advertising brand names, trademarks, etc.	Typically a great deal, particularly with product differentiation	Mostly public relations advertising
Examples	Agriculture	Retail trade, dresses, shoes	Steel, automobiles, farm implements, many household appliances	Local utilities

McConnell & Brue (2001, p. 462), indicates that the laws of supply and demand and the degrees of competition we can conclude the following, which can and will aid both established businesspeople and aspiring entrepreneurs in maintaining or growing their business:

a. The market models mentioned above are classifications into which most industries can be fitted with reasonable accuracy.

b. A purely competitive industry comprises a large number of independent firms producing a standardized product. Pure competition assumes that firms and resources are mobile among different industries.

c. No single firm can influence market price in a competitive industry. The firm's demand curve is perfectly elastic, and price therefore equals marginal revenue.

d. Short-run profit maximization by competitive firms can be analyzed by comparing total revenue and total cost or by conducting marginal analysis. A firm will maximize profits by producing that output at which total revenue exceeds total cost by the greatest amount. A business can maximize profits by producing where the excess of total cost over total revenue is a minimum and less than total fixed costs.

e. Provided that price exceeds minimum average variable cost, competitive firms will maximize profits or minimize losses in the short run by producing that output at which price or marginal revenue equals marginal cost. If price is less than average cost, the firm will minimize its losses by closing down. If price is greater than average cost, the firm will minimize its losses by producing more output. If price exceeds the average total cost, output will provide maximum economic profits for the firm.

f.   Generally, economists recognize four possible deterrents to allocating efficiency in a competitive economy.

    1.   There is no reason why the competitive market system will result in an optimal distribution of income.

    2.   In allocating resources, the competitive model does not allow for spillover costs and benefits or for the production of public goods.

    3.   A purely competitive industry may preclude the use of the best-known productive techniques and foster a slow rate of technological advancement.

    4.   A competitive system provides neither a wide range of product choice nor an environment conducive to the development of new products.

Key Terms

- **Average total cost**: The total cost of a firm divided by its output (the quantity of product produced); equal to average fixed cost plus average variable cost (McConnell & Brue, 2001, p. G2).

- **Average variable cost**: The total variable cost of a firm divided by its output (the quantity of product produced) (McConnell & Brue, 2001, p. G2).

- **Barrier to entry**: Anything that artificially prevents the entry of businesses into an industry (McConnell & Brue, 2001, p. G2).

- **Base year**: The year to which prices in other years are compared when a price index is constructed (McConnell & Brue, 2001, p. G2).

- **Bilateral monopoly**: A market in which there is a single seller (monopoly) and a single buyer (McConnell & Brue, 2001, p. G3).

- **Break-even income**: The level of disposable income at which households plan to consume (spend) all of their income (for consumer goods and services) and to save none of it; also denotes that level of earned income at which subsidy payments become zero in an income maintenance program (McConnell & Brue, 2001, p. G3).

- **Break-even point**: Any output that a firm might produce at which its total cost and total revenue would be equal; an output at which it has neither an economic profit nor a loss (McConnell & Brue, 2001, p. G3).

- **Business cycle**: Recurrent ups and down over a period of years in the level of economic activity (McConnell & Brue, 2001, p. G3).

- **Demographics**: Describes a population (Bangs & Pinson, 1999, p. 25).

- **Discount rate**: The interest rates Federal Reserve banks charge on the loans they make to depository institutions (McConnell & Brue, 2001, p. G7).

- **Disposable income**: Personal income less personal taxes; income available for personal consumption expenditures and personal saving (McConnell & Brue, 2001, p. G7).

- **Dis-saving**: Spending for consumer goods and services in excess of disposable income; the amount by which personal consumption expenditures exceed disposable income (McConnell & Brue, 2001, p. G8).

- **Durable good**: A consumer good with an expected life (period of usage) of one year or more (McConnell & Brue, 2001, p. G9).

- **Economies of scale**: The forces that reduce the average cost of producing a product as the firm expands the size of its plant (its output); in the long run, the economies of mass production (McConnell & Brue, 2001, p. G9).

- **Elasticity**: The interrelationship between demand and price (Bangs & Pinson, 1999, p. 25).

- **Fixed cost**: Any cost that in total does not change when a firm changes its output; the cost of fixed resources (McConnell & Brue, 2001, p. G11).

- **Homogeneous oligopoly**: An oligopoly in which firms produce a standardized product (McConnell & Brue, 2001, p. G13).

- **Interest**: The payment made for the use of money (of borrowed funds) (McConnell & Brue, 2001, p. G15).

- **Liquidity**: Assets that can be quickly and easily converted into money with little or no loss of purchasing power (McConnell & Brue, 2001, p. 17).

- **Mixed capitalism**: An economy in which both government and private decisions determine how resources are allocated (McConnell & Brue, 2001, p. G19).

Chapter 2

Economic Business Cycles: External Element

Learning Objectives:

- To learn the types of business cycles

- To learn the types of economic cycles

- To understand recession, depression, prosperity, and inflation

- To understand the impact of random events

Types of Business Cycles

Business cycles are periods during which a business, industry, or entire economy expands and contracts. Many business cycles are irregular, and business cycles encompass all aspects of an economy. A business cycle is felt in every nook and cranny of the economy. Few if any businesses escape the terrible faith of depression or the torrid faith of inflation. These economic storms are inescapable; however, the business cycle affects some industries in different ways and to different degrees. Business cycles vary in intensity and length, and they are sometimes based on seasons of the year, holidays, and other recurring events.

Economic business cycles, on the other hand, vary in length but usually follow a set pattern. They are not only unmistakable but also usually uncontrollable by a single business enterprise or entrepreneur. Examples of economic business cycles are prosperity, recession, depression, and recovery, all of which affect business enterprises and entrepreneurs. Many factors affect the business cycle, and businesses are either at its mercy or reap the benefits of the times. Usually, it takes a mass maneuver by local, state, and federal governments to boost or slow down the economic business cycle.

Expansions and contractions of the economy, sometimes referred to as booms and busts, are broad economic events that affect many industries and companies. According to Henricks (2001, p. 347), economic cycles generally adhere to the following ideas:

- Fluctuations tend to affect durable manufactured goods more than services

- Wholesale and industrial prices tend to be affected more than retail prices

- Short-term interest rates track and amplify the cycles, moving in an exaggerated manner along with the economy

We have already seen that business cycles affect the larger economy. These business cycles consist of expansions and contractions in a nation's aggregate economic activity. The contractions occur most obviously in the form of recessions, when growth slows across the economy. According to Henricks, "Expansions appear as booms, when a rising tide seems to lift all boats" (2001, p. 42). Timing is the problem. Economic cycles vary widely in terms of their length and severity. Expansions during peacetime in the United States average eighteen months to three years. Contractions run one to two years. The total cycle runs anywhere from two and a half to five years. According to Henricks, about the only thing you can count on is that expansions will usually be longer than contractions (2001, p. 43).

Economic Business Cycles Explained

The overall status of a national economy is usually cyclical and may be controlled by various techniques, depending on what phase of the economic cycle an economy is presently in. Following is an explanation of the economic cyles and an explanation of each.

Prosperity and inflation: Prosperity is an economic condition that exists when living standards are relatively high, unemployment is relatively low, and the economy is in an expansion phase. Production is high, people are spending their disposable income, and money is creating jobs and production throughout the economy. Prosperity and inflation is often defined as "too much money chasing too few goods" (Questia Media America, 2004). Most economies have not had much success in dealing with inflation. President Ford and President Carter have referred to it as "public enemy number one" (Wilson, 1982, p. 1).

Inflation is the biggest threat to stability (Ebert & Griffin, 2000, p. 19). Basically, it is a period of widespread price increases that occur throughout an economic system. Typically, inflation impacts all the goods and services that an economic system produces. Most inflations are initiated and sustained by an excess of spending in the economy as a whole. In other words, people, groups, businesses, government, and foreigners spend more or try to spend more than the economy can produce at full employment; in this case, prices in general will rise. In simpler terms, inflation is the relationship of total spending to total real output and capacity. Inflation is measured by price index numbers. A price index number measures the general level of prices in reference to a particular sector and to a base period. It is beyond the scope of this project to discuss the calculation procedure for developing the price index.

If persistent inflation occurs, resources will be allocated away from longer-term productive investments and toward assets. It is generally believed that the federal government can ensure high employment levels along with stable prices by skillfully adapting federal taxation and expenditure and by ensuring that the Federal Reserve carefully manages the money supply.

Entrepreneurs should understand that their sales revenue will be subject to peaks and valleys, depending on the current economic business cycle. The reality is that no business is insulated from industry cycles, economic trends, or seasonal fluctuations.

Ebert and Griffin note that inflation is not necessarily bad (2000, p. 18). After all, stability can degenerate into stagnation and contribute to a decline in the development and marketing of new products. When the market has enough material to produce and sell products at reasonable prices and customers have enough money with which to buy products, innovation and growth in new areas are not urgent business priorities. For this same reason, the onset of inflation is often a sign of economic growth. When businesses see that they can charge higher prices, they may hire more workers, invest more money in advertising, and introduce new products. New businesses open to take advantage of perceived prosperity.

Inflation cannot be controlled by the efforts of a single business enterprise. However, it can be curtailed both naturally and artificially, such as by controlling interest rates; in this case, an increase in interest by the federal government may slow the buying momentum and, therefore, the economy. Since too much of a slowdown will create a recession, the federal government must conduct a delicate balancing act. When the government creates too much money, an inflationary boom is generated; a relative paucity of money will precipitate a declining output and unemployment, known as a recession or depression (McConnell & Brue, 2001, p. 131).

Recession and depression: A recession is the contraction phase of a business cycle, a period of a relatively low volume of production and income in an economy. Inflation is not the only threat to economic stability. If the unemployment level rises, the unemployed will reduce their spending, causing a chain reaction. Local businesses will suffer drops in sales and perhaps cut their own workforces. The resulting event will be a recession, characterized by decreases in employment, income, and production. A particularly severe and long-lasting recession, such as the one that affected much of the country in the 1930s, is called a depression.

Although businesses have little control over business cycles, a sensible growth plan takes into account the cycles of business and finds ways to minimize and exploit them (Henricks, 2001, p. 346).

According to Ebert & Griffin, nearly all economic systems have three broad goals: stability, full employment, and growth (2000, p. 18). There are different approaches to achieving these goals, and each business cycle affects these goals differently.

Random Events: External Elements

External elements like wars, floods, and fires can have powerful effects on business enterprises. Pure random events, such as hurricanes, droughts, and earthquakes, simonies, and fires, can also affect the economy and, as a result, affect the business enterprise and the entrepreneur. Although these effects tend to be negative, some events, particularly wars, tend to affect the entire economy, producing booms in their early years as government spending mushrooms. Many companies have built their businesses on lucrative defense contracts obtained during wartime. However, these booms are usually followed by the dampening effect of inflation and, later, recession, as the economy cools down (Henricks, 200, p. 348). Businesses should not hope for disaster; rather, they should be ready to leap into action when random events create extra demand for their products and services.

A lot of effort has been expended in trying to develop ways of predicting business cycles. However, few elements are really agreed upon. The stock market, interest rates, price indices, new housing construction, the automobile industry, and the unemployment rate have all been used as indicators to predict the next business cycle. Again, however, random events are external elements that a business enterprise can react to but not prevent.

It may seem like a given that the best time to grow is when the economic business cycle is on the upswing. Indeed, this is true if your business is the kind that can ramp up production or change direction quickly. But if you are in an industry that requires longer lead times for planning, you may need to begin your growth effort when market and business cycles are at the bottom or just beginning to trend down. The important thing to note is that you should not start your growth plan without making an effort to synchronize it with cycles that are larger than the business (Henricks, 2001, p. 45).

A tremendous amount of effort has been expended over the years in attempting to predict the occurrences of business cycles. Reaching a consensus has always been difficult. Experts generally cannot agree on what issues may be precursors of downturns, such as falling stock prices, profit margins, and profit potential (Henricks, 2001, p. 348), and they disagree on the timing of these so-called leading indicators. According to Henricks, it may be weeks or months after a stock market crash before the economy begins to show signs of receding—and it may never happen at all. There are, however, other indicators that economists may turn to for help in tracking and forecasting changes in the business cycle, such as housing starts, interest rates, and price indices—but possibly to no avail (2001, p. 349).

Key Terms

- **Business enterprise**: An organization that provides goods or services to earn profits (Ebert & Griffin, 2000, p. 482).

- **Consumer goods**: Products purchased by consumers for personal use (Ebert & Griffin, 2000, p. 482).

- **Depression:** A severe and long-lasting recession (Ebert & Griffin, 2000, p. 483).

- **Derived demand**: Demand for industrial products that results from demand for consumer products (Ebert & Griffin, 2000, p. 483).

- **Direct-response retailing:** Nonstore retailing by direct interaction with customers to inform them of products and elicit sales orders (Ebert & Griffin, 2000, p. 484).

- **Dow-Jones Industrial Average:** A market index based on the prices of thirty of the largest industrial firms listed on the NYSE (Ebert & Griffin, 2000, p. 484).

- **Monopolistic competition:** A market or industry characterized by numerous buyers and relatively numerous sellers trying to differentiate their products from those of competitors (Ebert & Griffin, 2000, p. 487).

- **National debt:** The total amount a nation owes its creditors (Ebert & Griffin, 2000, p. 487).

- **Pricing objectives:** Goals that producers hope to attain in pricing products for sale (Ebert & Griffin, 2000, p. 488).

- **Revenues:** Funds that flow into a business from the sale of goods or services (Ebert & Griffin, 2000, p. 489).

Chapter 3

You and Your Family: Internal Element

Learning Objectives:

- To determine if entrepreneurship is right for you

- To determine the definition of an entrepreneur

- To determine if there is an entrepreneurial archetype

- To understand the important role the family plays in the success of a business

- To learn what it takes to be a success

- To learn how to define success

- To understand the importance of self-evaluation

- To identify the attributes of successful entrepreneurs

- To recognize errors in judgment and avoid them to promote business success

Entrepreneurs play a vital role in America's economic structure. Colleges and universities report that the most popular courses in their business administration departments concern entrepreneurship and emerging firms (Calmes, 2003, pp.1-3).

As a result of the tremendous interest in the entrepreneurial route, numerous books have been written on the so-called entrepreneurial spirit, and many research groups are focused on what is believed to be the entrepreneurial archetype. Their studies attempt to determine if a budding entrepreneur has the internal elements required to succeed in the business world.

Do you have the attributes and characteristics of an entrepreneur? Today's researchers believe that some of the necessary traits for successful entrepreneurs are drive, commitment, passion, energy, leadership, and pride of ownership (Calmes, 2003, p. 1.3).

Common sense dictates that before we continue the discussion about entrepreneurs and growing a business enterprise, we should establish a firm, clear definition of an entrepreneur.

Definition of Entrepreneur

The intent of this section is to establish a definition of "entrepreneur," which will be used throughout this project.

To begin to understand entrepreneurship's benefit to business, it is important to first define the term itself. Ever since the term "entrepreneurship" was established in the 1700s, researchers have debated its definition (National Commission on Entrepreneurship [NCOE], 1999). It is often defined as the ability and willingness to undertake the organization and management of production (Anderson, 2003). Entrepreneurship is often associated with the functions of innovating and bearing risks, in addition to making the usual business decisions (Anderson, 2003). Entrepreneurship is also defined as a function involving the exploitation of opportunities that exist within a market (Brillo, 2000). Such exploitation is most commonly associated with the direction and/or combination of productive inputs (Brillo, 2000). Entrepreneurs usually bear risk while pursuing opportunities; however, their risks are usually calculated and well thought out. Often entrepreneurs are associated with creative and innovative actions (Kautz, 1999). Though entrepreneurs undertake a managerial role in their activities, routine management of an ongoing operation is not considered to be entrepreneurship (Brillo, 1999). In this sense, entrepreneurial activity is said to be fleeting. An individual may perform an entrepreneurial function in creating an organization, but he or she may later be relegated to the role of managing it without performing an entrepreneurial role. In this sense, many small-business owners would not be considered entrepreneurs. Finally, individuals within organizations can be classified as entrepreneurs because they pursue the exploitation of opportunities (Anderson, 2003; Brillo, 1999; Kautz, 1999; Mador, 2000). However, it should be noted that those employees are referred to as intrepraneurs.

Although much has been written about entrepreneurship, the material is fragmented and controversial. The same is true concerning the definition of "entrepreneur," which is generally defined as "an organizer or promoter of an activity, or one that manages and assumes the risk of a business."

Despite such a formal definition, confusion exists about the actual meaning of the term. Some use the term to refer to the owners of all small businesses, while others use the term to refer to the owners of all new businesses. In reality, however, many well-established businesses engage in highly successful entrepreneurial endeavors, and the owners may not be considered entrepreneurs. This omission exists because they did not found the business and were not originally involved in its development (Timmons, 1999, p. 6). The term "entrepreneur," then, refers not only to an enterprise's size or age but also to the nature of the businessperson's primary involvement in the enterprise.

Many people long perceived as successful entrepreneurs would not fit some of the proposed definitions. Self-employed individuals and business proprietors may be surprised and offended to learn that some academics and researchers, such as Timmons and Fasiska, would suggest that they are not really entrepreneurs but merely small-business owners (Timmons, 1999, p. 5; Fasiska, 1994, p. 1).

Austrian economist Joseph Schumpter defines entrepreneurship as placing an emphasis on innovation, such as new products, new production methods, new markets, or new forms of organization (Mador, 2000). Wealth is created when such innovation results in new demand. Many people use the terms "entrepreneur" and "small-business owner" synonymously. The two terms have much in common, but there are significant differences between their ventures, including the following:

- Amount of wealth created: Rather than just creating an income stream, successful entrepreneurial ventures create substantial wealth, typically in excess of several million dollars.

- Speed of wealth creation: While a successful small business can generate several million dollars of profit over a lifetime, entrepreneurial wealth creation is often rapid, sometimes occurring within five years.

- Risk: The risk of an entrepreneurial venture must be high; otherwise, with the incentive of sure profits, many entrepreneurs would be pushing the idea, and the opportunity would no longer exist.

- Innovation: Entrepreneurship often involves substantial innovation beyond what a small business might exhibit. This innovation gives the venture the competitive advantage that results in wealth creation. The innovation may be in the product or

service itself or in the business processes used to deliver it (Mador, 2000, p. 2).

Low (2001) and Low and Macmillan (1988) assert the following:

> The problem with these definitions is that though each captures an aspect of entrepreneurship, none captures the whole picture. The phenomenon of entrepreneurship is intertwined with a complex set of contiguous and overlapping constructs such as management of change, innovation, technological and environmental turbulence. (Low & Macmillan, 1988, p. 141)

Low (2001) continues to argue for a broader look at entrepreneurship. He

reports that research on entrepreneurship is still in its adolescence and has much room for

further development. He reported:

> Over the past decade, significant research efforts have been expended, as is evidenced by the proliferation of entrepreneurship journals, professional associations, conferences, meetings, and academic appointments. This flurry of activity has brought significant attention to the field, but only a modest level of academic legitimacy. (p. 18).

Most research has agreed that entrepreneurs fall into four categories:

(Anderson, 2003; Brillo, 1999; Kautz, 1999)

- Entrepreneurs who use innovation to improve the quality of life

- Entrepreneurs who create new jobs

- Entrepreneurs who improve a country's position in the global economic

  competition

- Entrepreneurs who create economic growth and new wealth for reinvestment in

  their country (NCOE, 1999, p. 2)

Marvilla (2000) offers a composite profile of America's entrepreneurs based on

an analysis of the Consumer Population Survey by the U.S. Census Bureau. According to these data, there were approximately 12.8 million self-employed people nationwide in 2000. The self-employed are typically married (about 74 percent of the sample) and white (about 90 percent of the sample). Males dominate the entrepreneurial landscape, making up 65.6 percent of the total number of self-employed people. Entrepreneurs overwhelmingly belong to the broad age group of twenty-five to fifty-nine; about 82 percent of the sample fell between those ages. Thirty percent (30 percent) of the self-employed are in their forties, while people in their thirties and fifties each represent slightly under a quarter of the self-employed. The majority of entrepreneurs work for their business on a full-time basis. About 70 percent of the self-employed have family incomes of $25,000 or higher and about 28 percent have incomes of over $75,000. Most of those who started their own businesses are well educated. About 60 percent have received at least some college education, and, according to the National Association for the Self-Employed (NASE), about 24 percent of their members hold a bachelor's degree, versus only 16.5 percent of all Americans over the age of twenty-five (Marvilla, 2000, p. 3).

Categories of Entrepreneurship

According to Anderson (2003), there are two important categories to mention when discussing entrepreneurship and its role in business development: small businesses and micro-enterprises. These two categories do not describe all entrepreneurial enterprises, but they do encompass the largest share of businesses that fit within the definition of entrepreneurship. What follows is a brief discussion of those two types.

Small businesses: The SBA has various definitions for small businesses, depending on the type of industry (Anderson, 2003). Manufacturing and mining businesses with fewer than five hundred employees are considered small businesses, while businesses in wholesale trade industries must have fewer than one hundred employees. For other industries, such as retail and construction, businesses are classified based on annual revenues (SBA, 2002). According to Anderson, "There are approximately 25 million small businesses in the country, which currently employ more than half of the country's workforce and account for more than half of the private sector economic output" (2003, p. 1). Small businesses provide approximately 75 percent of the new jobs added to the economy (NASE, no date).

Even though small businesses aren't all growing enterprises, their flexible nature allows them to quickly develop and adapt new products, services, and technologies and to create and enter new market niches and business models. As larger, more established firms are generally less likely than smaller, entrepreneurially oriented enterprises to reward innovation or to experiment with risky new ventures, they are less likely to promote the new ideas, technologies, and business methods that will lead to economic growth in the twenty-first century (Anderson, 2003, p. 2).

Anderson further states that the health of small businesses is of critical importance to any nation's economic stability. Small businesses lead to new innovations and are responsible for creating many new jobs.

Micro-enterprises: Anderson defines a micro-enterprise as a business with fewer than five employees that requires less than $35,000 in start-up money. There are nearly two million micro-entrepreneurs in the United States today, and the micro-enterprise sector is growing daily. Micro-enterprises vary in type but range from cleaning services and childcare programs to designer textiles and specialty foods. These businesses often employ members of the same family and sometimes grow into larger businesses that employ others in the community (Association for Enterprise Opportunity, 2002).

Brill (1999) points out:

One of the most promising economic development strategies for low-income communities in the United States that has emerged in the past decade is micro-enterprise. Micro-enterprise is entrepreneurship on the small scale that offers the most disadvantaged an escape from the trap of minimum wage jobs or welfare. (p. 1)

Though research on micro-enterprises is relatively new, existing research suggests that the micro-enterprise is an important element of entrepreneurship. Dumas (1999) reported the following about micro-entrepreneurs:

- Micro-entrepreneurs are relatively well-educated: 83 percent are high school graduates, 58 percent have some education beyond high school, 19 percent have four-year college degrees, and 8 percent have graduate degrees.

- A typical micro-enterprise is a sole proprietorship that has been in operation for two or more years, with sales of less than $12,000 per year. Most micro-businesses are in wholesale or retail trade or services, as well as some manufacturing and construction firms.

- Over time, micro-businesses show high survival rates (78 percent), gains in net worth, and employment generation. Profitability over time fluctuates.

- The majority of low-income micro-entrepreneurs show income gains over time (55 percent), and 25 percent had income gains large enough to move out of poverty. (cited in Dumas, 1999, p. 4)

Selecting the appropriate basis for defining and understanding the entrepreneurial person is certainly a worthy challenge for academic researchers and writers. There is generally no accepted definition or model of what an entrepreneur is or does. All of these factors tend to cause confusion about the meaning of "entrepreneur."

A tremendous amount of literature has been developed on the subject, ranging from academic studies to blueprints for setting up new ventures. The term "entrepreneur" has often been applied to the founder of a new business (Timmons, 1999, p. 5). Given this interpretation, anyone who inherits a business, such as Henry Ford III; buys a business, such as George Steinbrenner; or manages a business and turns that business around, such as Lee Iacocca, is by many definitions not an entrepreneur (Cunningham, 1991, p. 45).

Due to the vast range of viewpoints, it is not surprising that a consensus on the definition of "entrepreneurship" has not been reached. Cunningham describes six schools of thought regarding entrepreneurship and attempts to show how they may be useful for understanding and defining the entrepreneurship process. The six models of entrepreneurship are the following:

1. The Great Person School of Entrepreneurship: The central focus of the model is that the entrepreneur has an intuitive ability or a sixth sense that he or she was born with.

2.   The Psychological Characteristics School: This school of thought contends that entrepreneurs have unique values, attitudes, and needs that drive them.

3.   The Classical School of the Entrepreneurial Model: Cunningham reserves this category for the creative activity of the innovator. This definition excludes the majority of those pursuing entrepreneurial and business activities. Others even refer to the identification and exploitation of an opportunity as entrepreneurial.

4.   The Management School: This school is focused on the fact that entrepreneurs are organizers of an economic venture. They are people who organize, own, manage, and assume the risk.

5.   The Leadership School: This category suggests that entrepreneurs are leaders of people; they have the ability to adapt their style to the needs of different people.

6.   The Intrapreneurship School: This category recognizes that entrepreneurial skills can be useful in complex organizations.

Cunningham (1991), suggests that it may not be prudent to assume that knowledge of entrepreneurs can be obtained by focusing on the criteria of only one model. An understanding of entrepreneurs and their ventures requires criteria from each facet of the overall process: entrepreneurs, personal perspective, their ways of identifying opportunities, their methods of acting and managing, and their mechanisms for adapting and reassessing (Cunningham, 1991, p. 58).

A panel of business editors, economists, and educators has defined "entrepreneur" as "the originator or the principal mover of an enterprise." Such entrepreneurs are characterized by a willingness to take risks and to invest money and energy in the development of a product or service as contributors of value to the enterprise. *Business*

Week's "1993 Special Issue on Entrepreneurs" defines entrepreneurs as "owners" who reap the rewards if they are successful and suffer the consequences if they fail (O'Neal, p. 250).

Timmons, in his book *The Entrepreneurial Mind* (1999), presents a working definition of entrepreneurship as "the pursuit of opportunity without regard to resources you currently control" (p. 16). He credits this definition to Howard Stevenson and others at the Harvard Business School (1999, p. 17).

Schell (1993) believes that an entrepreneur "doesn't care much about information or facts. He is liable to operate from instinct" (p. 241). Schell also indicates that many people become entrepreneurs accidentally, stumbling into ventures haphazardly. This entrepreneur's primary purpose is survival rather than growth (Schell, 1993, p. 242). Again, such people may consider themselves entrepreneurs; however, according to some criteria, they are merely working people. Because of these reasons, some researchers are endeavoring to clearly define the term "entrepreneur" and refine it for consistency. The definition of entrepreneurship has evolved over the past few years thanks to work done at the Harvard Business School and Babson College. Here entrepreneurship is defined as "creating and building something of value from practically nothing" (Timmons, 1999, pp. 17–19). Also, according to Timmons, entrepreneurship involves personal energy expended by initiating and building an enterprise or organization, rather than by being involved as an outside spectator (1999, p. 5).

Given the numerous definitions of entrepreneurship and the numerous profiles of an entrepreneur, for the purposes of this project, entrepreneur will be defined as follows: "A person who has founded or takes over his or her own enterprise, creates additional value to it, and manages it." Although there are numerous criteria for measuring the success of an enterprise, it is well known that most businesses disappear in the first few years. For that reason, remaining viable in these difficult initial years would certainly mean success for the founder/entrepreneur.

Self-Evaluation

The entrepreneurial journey begins with the desire and passion to transform a dream of business ownership into reality. Self-evaluation is crucial to the process of actualizing this dream. You must examine your motivation, interest, character, and goals to determine whether owning a business will bring you joy or grief. In the process, you can decide whether or not you are meant to be an entrepreneur.

You are the purpose and motivation for this effort, and it is important that you clearly define your interest, character, goals, and anything else that concerns you. The objective of this chapter is to help you determine if entrepreneurship is for you and identify the attributes and characteristics of successful entrepreneurs. After reading this chapter, you will be ready to start your entrepreneurial journey.

Once you have begun an entrepreneurial endeavor, it can be scary to find out that entrepreneurship is not for you or your family. I include family because I want to make it perfectly clear that if your spouse or other family members are not behind you and cannot provide the necessary support, then perhaps your venture should wait for another time.

Owning a small business is not an ordinary effort; it is a unique experience. You must ask yourself whether you are ready to commit to making your dream a reality. Your commitment will be to your business and your business alone. You will probably have less time for your personal life, and you may be using much of what you own as collateral to raise the funds for starting your business.

All ventures and all decisions have pros and cons, and starting your own business is certainly no different. Some of the pros and cons of becoming an entrepreneur that I have discovered through my many years of experience are listed in the sections that follow.

Pros

- Starting a business will be one of the most rewarding challenges you will ever undertake.

- You will have the chance to make more money than you could possibly make working for someone else.

- You will have the opportunity to experience the feeling of achievement.

- You will learn about every aspect of a business and gain experience in a variety of disciplines.

- You will have the opportunity to work directly with customers.

- You will become your own boss and make decisions that are crucial to the success or failure of the business.

- You cannot be fired by anyone except you yourself.

- You will have the chance to put ideas into practice.

- You will participate in every aspect of running a business.

- You will be able to benefit the local economy by hiring other people within the community.

- You will be able to work in a field or area you really enjoy.

- You will have the opportunity to create your own wealth.

- You will have the opportunity to plant roots in a community and give your family a sense of belonging and stability.

- You can provide a future for your children if they wish to follow in your footsteps.

Cons

- Being an entrepreneur is one of the most difficult challenges you will undertake.

- You may have to take a large financial risk.

- You will probably have to work long hours and may have fewer opportunities to take vacations.

- You may have to neglect your family.

- You will neglect your personal needs.

- You will neglect the things you really enjoy.

- You may become ill, and, if you do, your business will suffer.

- You may find that your income is not steady; your cash flow may suffer.

- You will have to do things you will not like, such as firing an employee.

- You will be responsible for making sure your workers are able to earn a living.

- You will have to make hundreds of decisions each and every day. Although some decisions may be wrong, the majority of them must be on track.

The goal of an entrepreneur is to be successful. To accomplish this goal, he or she must carefully select and evaluate key business objectives. Next, he or she must prepare a viable plan for achieving the goals. These actions are crucial to the success of an enterprise.

To create a business from scratch and succeed at it, an entrepreneur must have motivation and perseverance bordering on obsession. Owning a business may require you to be ruthless to yourself, your family, and your friends; you might be considered antisocial, and such an obsession may negatively impact your personal life and family relationships. However, an entrepreneur accepts all this and more; it is the price of success.

Self-evaluation can help you determine if self-employment is a desirable path for you. To be a successful entrepreneur, you must examine whether you are capable of change. Such an understanding is a necessary starting point and a strong basis on which to build; it will allow you to see what you could be and decide whether you can grow in that image. Not all aspiring entrepreneurs can accomplish such objective self-examination, but the process can be a useful guide. You can uncover who you are now and what you can become tomorrow.

Defining Success

Now that you have clarified your idea of what makes a successful entrepreneur, we will examine what the experts have to say.

Everyone loves a winner—we have all heard this at one time or another. But what is a successful person or a successful entrepreneur? Well, success is relative; it depends on how you look at it. It depends on whether you are satisfied with yourself, and it depends on how other people look at you. It is safe to say that success is relative and that it rests solely with what makes a person comfortable with him or herself. Maybe your joys and fears have found you; maybe you are still in business, succeeding beyond your wildest dreams. In short, you and your business are a success. Cool, you succeeded.

You have undoubtedly put in long hours, suffered numerous trials, and dug into your soul more deeply than you ever thought possible. As a business owner, you recognize the hard work and commitment it takes to keep a business going. Your status is well earned; you are a success, and you should soak in the glory of this success. However, keep in mind that success has its own sets of traps that can undo all your hard work. The biggest trap is forgetting that success can disappear as fast as it appeared. Here today, gone tomorrow.

But what is success, exactly? As noted earlier, success is relative and can mean different things to different people. To some people, a successful entrepreneur is someone whose business has survived over a period of time. For others, success is any business that is surviving at any time.

What It Takes to Become a Success

According to Dave Thomas, the founder of Wendy's International, "Success all starts with a dream. The hardest part of becoming a success is being willing to do whatever it takes to make your dream a reality" (cited in Norman, 1999, p. 3). Thomas also offers some basic rules for achieving success:

- Do your research. Know the business you want to start. Understand your customers and their needs.

- Your dream must be different in some way from your competitors' dreams.

- Quality and customer service must be your twin top priorities.

- You must work hard. Research has indicated that Dave Thomas's advice about hard work is almost universally accepted among successful entrepreneurs (Stolze, 2000).

Thomas emphasizes two important elements of success:

1. If you do not have a burning desire to succeed, you will not.

2. When you do succeed, it is very important that you give back to your community, (Norman, 1999, p. 3).

Regardless of how you enter the business arena—whether it is by purchasing an existing business, purchasing a franchise, undertaking a multi-level marketing, or starting a business from scratch you must have a vision and a dream and be willing to work hard. In addition, you must be fully prepared so the odds of success are in your favor.

All new businesses are a game of survival, and surviving is a struggle over the long run. Surviving in business is like walking through a swamp or forest where you face an obstacle with every step. If you allow the obstacles to defeat you, your business will fail. Indeed, many students of entrepreneurship ascribe these failures to "errors in judgment."

Mancuso points out that those errors in judgment account for many business failures (1993, p. 129). Many errors in judgment occur in the initial stage and encompass the following:

1. The wrong location

2. The wrong product line

3. Insufficient capital

4. Not planning before the venture or doing enough homework

5. Opening the wrong business in the wrong place

6. Poor strategy in running the business

Some businesses fail because of factors relating to the commitment of the business owner, such as the following:

7. Lack of involvement in the business or neglect in the operation of the business

8. Lack of concern for operating expenses

9. Lack of concern for debt service

10. Poor work habits, such as lack of attention to business, neatness, caring, and punctuality

11. Lack of commitment to the business, customers, suppliers, and employees

12. Fraudulent actions toward the customers, employers, or government

Other reasons for failure are related to the personal environment, such as the following:

13. Poor health of the major owners

14. Lack of total support from immediate family members, such as spouse or children

15. Business conflicts, such as operating more than one business or working and running a business

16. Family problems, such as illness or financial hardship

According to Mariotti, no one is born with all the characteristics needed for success. If you lack some of the required characteristics but have substantial energy and motivation, you can develop the needed traits (internal elements). Listed below are a dozen of the traits generally considered most important for businesses. Think about which ones you could develop with a little effort (Mariotti, 2000, p. 78):

1.   Adaptability: The ability to cope with new situations and find creative solutions to problems

2.   Competitiveness: The willingness to compete with and test oneself against others

3.   Confidence: The belief that you can do what you set out to do

4.   Discipline: The ability to stay focused and stick to a schedule and deadlines

5.   Drive: The desire to work hard to accomplish your goals

6.   Honesty: The commitment to tell the truth and deal with people fairly

7.   Organization: The ability to structure your life and keep tasks and information in order

8.   Perseverance: The refusal to quit; the willingness to keep goals in sight and work toward them despite obstacles

9.   Persuasiveness: The knack for convincing people to see your point of view and to get them interested in your ideas

10. Risk taking: The courage to expose yourself to possible losses

11. Understanding: The ability to listen to and empathize with other people

12. Vision: The ability to see the end results of your goals while working to achieve them

According to Stolze (1999), personal qualities not found in successful entrepreneurs are compulsive gambling, high risk taking, and compulsive snap decision making (p. 20). In addition, factors Stolze deems to be irrelevant are gender, marital status, and educational level (p. 23).

According to Burnstiner (1996), to increase the chance for survival and success, an entrepreneur should do the following:

1. Prepare him or her for the challenge by obtaining a good education, preferably one that includes some business courses.

2. Accumulate months or even years of experience in the field he or she is seeking to enter.

3. Secure a managerial post in the target field to gain as much exposure as possible to the many facets of business operations, including sales, purchasing, production, inventory, control, and financial management.

4. Keep up with industry changes and innovations by reading business and trade publications and using personal contacts.

In essence, all of the elements listed above can be categorized into five essential ingredients that lead to successful entrepreneurship (Burstiner, 1999, p. 4):

1. A qualified entrepreneur

2. A potential business opportunity

3. A solid and detailed plan

4. Sufficient capital

5. Luck

Burstiner (1999) also proposes other personal qualities that appear to Characterize most individuals who operate a successful business (Burstiner, 1999, p. 9):

- Energy

- Imagination

- Good health

- Self-control

- Timing

- Confidence

- Boldness

- Independence

- Empathy

- Self-discipline

- Innovation

- Consideration

- Ethics

- Tact

- Good judgment

- Adaptability

- Sociability

From what we have presented thus far, we can conclude that a successful entrepreneur fulfills the following requirements:

1. Willing to work hard

2. Can get along well with others

3. Is willing to accept the challenges

4. Welcomes responsibility

5. Is a self-starter

6. Is willing and able to make decisions

7. Knows how to form a team

8. Knows how to organize

Several studies address the subject of successfully operating a business. There are also many books and self-evaluation tests that are concerned with determining one's aptitude for being an entrepreneur. According to Gillis (1999) none of these tests are more than 85 percent correct, and none can measure the guts or the "fire in the belly" (p. 8).

If the characteristics and attributes listed in this chapter describe you, you're a candidate for starting your own business. If they do not, you can utilize the information to improve your future business potential and your status at your present job. Employees can strengthen their job security by becoming valued—that is, they add value to a business. Entrepreneurs build their business on the merits of their valued employees. An employee will probably always have a good job if he or she can portray him or her as a valued employee.

Key Terms

- **Amortization:** To liquidate on an installment basis; the process of gradually paying off a liability over a period of time. For example, a mortgage is amortized by periodically paying off part of the face amount of the mortgage (Bangs & Pinson, 1999, p. 629).

- **Business venture:** Taking financial risks in a commercial enterprise (Bangs & Pinson, 1999, p. 630).

- **Distributor:** Middleman, wholesaler, agent, or company distributing goods to dealers or companies (Bangs & Pinson, 1999, p. 629).

- **Financial statements:** Periodic reports that summarize the financial affairs of a business (Bangs & Pinson, 1999, p. 633).

- **Franchise**: A business that requires three elements: a franchise fee, a common trade name, and a continuous relationship with the parent company (Bangs &

Pinson, 1999, p. 634).

- **Intrapreneurship**: The development of independent units to create, market, and expand services (Cunningham, 1991, p. 49).

- **Lifestyle:** A pattern of living that comprises an individual's activities, interests, and opinions (Bangs & Pinson, 1999, p. 635).

- **Small business**: An enterprise that reflects the following characteristics (Burnstine (Anderson, 2003; Brillo, 1999; Kautz, 1999 p.15): independently owned and operated; localized scope of operations; not dominant in its field; and of relatively small size for a particular industry.

- **Venture capitalist:** A risk taker and professional opportunity seeker. Venture capitalists usually specialize in certain industries and prefer newer companies that have demonstrated high growth potential. Such companies usually offer higher-than-average profits to their shareholders (Bangs & Pinson, 1999, pp. 159–160).

Chapter 4

The Entrepreneur's Quiz: Internal Element

Learning Objectives:

- To evaluate your entrepreneurial attributes and characteristics

- To identify the factors involved in business success and failure

- To recognize the ingredients for successful entrepreneurship

Researchers have attempted to determine the traits that characterize entrepreneurs. Although no comprehensive list of attributes exists, studies have shown that there are certain general characteristics and attributes that successful entrepreneurs seem to possess.

Most entrepreneurial research has focused on the influence that genes, family, education, and career experience have on an entrepreneur. Successful entrepreneurs seem to be of both sexes and of every imaginable size, shape, color, and description. However, no psychological model has been developed (Mancuso, 1993, p. 16). The central question is, "How do entrepreneurs become successful?" Successful entrepreneurs share common characteristics, attitudes, and behaviors. They all seem to work hard, are driven by intense commitment, and are determined to persevere. They see the cup as half full rather than as half empty (p. 14).

Dr. McCelland, in his book *The Achieving Society* (1961), has determined that entrepreneurs are driven by the need to achieve rather than by money. Please note that although McCelland may seem dated, this research is considered a core insight into the characteristics and attributes of a successful entrepreneur.

While there is an undeniable core of inborn characteristics (for example, energy and raw intelligence) that an entrepreneur either has or does not have, it is becoming apparent that such inborn traits combine with other attributes and characteristics to create a successful entrepreneur. There is no predetermined entrepreneurial model. However, there are certain character traits that indicate an entrepreneurial personality (Mancuso, 1993, p. 20).

In this chapter, you will find a quiz that was developed from a series of questionnaires administered by the Center for Entrepreneurial Management. Founded in 1978, the Center is the world's largest nonprofit association; its founder and CEO is Joseph R. Mancuso. This quiz and its answers were drawn from Mancuso's book *How to start, finance, and manage your own small business (rev. ed.)* (1993). Dr. Mancusco was gracious enough to grant me permission to use this quiz.

Please note that there are many entrepreneurial quizzes that are very sophisticated and complicated. I have chosen this one because of the apparent validity and reliability of the results. Although it may seem outdated, in my estimation it has withstood the test of time. Please see **Table 4** for the Entrepreneur's Quiz.

Table 4: Entrepreneur's Quiz

Source: Mancuso, J. (1993). *How to start, finance, and manage your own small business.* New York: Simon & Schuster. pp. 17–24. Reprinted with permission.

1.   How were your parents employed?

        a. Both worked and were self-employed for most of their working lives.

b. Both worked and were self-employed for some part of their working lives.

c. One parent was self-employed for most of his or her working life.

d. One parent was self-employed at some point in his or her working life.

e. Neither parent was ever self-employed.

2. Have you ever been fired from a job?

    a. Yes, more than once.

    b. Yes, once.

    c. No.

3. Are you an immigrant, or were your parents or grandparents immigrants?

    a. I was born outside of the U.S.

    b. One or both of my parents were born outside of the U.S.

    c. At least one of my grandparents was born outside of the U.S.

    d. Does not apply.

4. Your work career has been?

    a. Primarily in small business (under 100 employees).

    b. Primarily in medium-sized business (100-500 employees).

    c. Primarily in big business (over 500 employees).

5. Did you operate any businesses before you were twenty?

    a. Many

    b. A few

    c. None

6. What is your present age?

    a. 21–30

    b. 31–40

    c. 41–50

    d. 51 or over

7. You are the _____ child in the family.

    a. Oldest

    b. Middle

    c. Youngest

8. You are:

    a. Married

b. Divorced

c. Single

9.   Your highest level of formal education is:

     a. Some high school.

     b. High school diploma.

     c. Bachelor's degree.

     d. Master's degree.

     e. Doctor's degree.

10.   What is your primary motivation in starting a business?

     a. To make money.

     b. I don't like working for someone else.

     c. To be famous.

     d. As an outlet for excess energy.

11.   Your relationship to the parent who provided most of the family's income was:

     a. Strained

     b. Comfortable

     c. Competitive

     d. Non-existent

12.   You find the answers to difficult questions by:

     a. Working hard.

     b. Working smart.

     c. Both.

13.   On whom do you rely for critical management advice?

     a. Internal management teams.

     b. External management professionals.

     c. External financial professionals.

     d. No one except myself.

14.   If you were at the racetrack, which of these could you bet on?

     a. The daily double: A chance to make a killing.

     b. A 10:1 shot.

     c. A 3:1 shot.

     d. The 2:1 favorite.

15.   The only ingredient that is both necessary and sufficient for starting a business is:

        a. Money.
        b. Customers.
        c. An idea or product.
        d. Motivation and hard work.

16.   At a cocktail party, you:

        a. Are the life of the party.
        b. Never know what to say to people.
        c. Just fit into the crowd.

17.   You tend to "fall in love" too quickly with:

        a. New product ideas.
        b. New employees.
        c. New manufacturing ideas.
        d. New financial plans
        e. All of the above.

18.   Which of the following personality types is best suited to be your right-hand person?

        a. Bright and energetic.
        b. Bright and lazy.
        c. Dumb and energetic.

19.   You accomplish tasks better because:

        a. You are always on time.
        b. You are super organized.
        c. You keep good records.
        d. You have someone else do the work.

20.   You hate to discuss:

        a. Problems involving employees.
        b. Signing expense practices.
        c. New management practices.
        d. The future of the business.

21.   Given a choice, you would prefer:

a. Rolling dice with a 1:3 chance of winning.
b. Working on a problem with a 1:3 chance of solving it in the time allocated.

22.   If you could choose between the following competitive professions, your choice would be:

a. Professional golf.
b. Sales.
c. Personnel counseling.
d. Teaching.

23.   If you had to choose between working with a partner who is a close friend and working with a stranger who is an expert in your field, you would choose:

a. The close friend.
b.   The expert.

24.   In business situations that demand action clarifying who is in charge will help produce results.
a. Agree.
b. Agree, with reservations.
c. Disagree.

25.   In playing a competitive game, you are concerned with:

a. How well you play.
b. Winning or losing.
c. Both of the above.
d. Neither of the above.

Please turn to the next page for the scoring process. Add up your score on the next page and compare it to the evaluation, also on the next page.

Table 5

Question 1 a = 10 b = 5 c = 5 d = 2	Question 8 a = 10 b = 2 c = 2	Question 14 a = 0 b = 2 c = 10	Question 20 a = 8 b = 10 c = 0 d = 0
Question 2 a = 10 b = 7 c = 0	Question 9 a = 2 b = 3 c = 10 d = 8 e = 4	Question 15 a = 0 b = 10 c = 0 d = 0	Question 21 a = 0 b = 15
Question 3 a = 5 b = 4 c = 3 d = 0	Question 10 a = 0 b = 15 c = 0 d = 0	Question 16 a = 0 b = 10 c = 3 d = 0	Question 22 a = 3 b = 10 c = 0 d = 0
Question 4 a = 10 b = 5 c = 0	Question 11 a = 10 b = 5 c = 10 d = 5	Question 17 a = 5 b = 5 c = 5 d = 5	Question 23 a = 0 b = 10
Question 5 a = 10 b = 7 c = 0	Question 12 a = 0 b = 5 c = 10	Question 18 a = 2 b = 10 c = 0	Question 24 a = 10 b = 2 c = 0
Question 6 a = 8 b = 10 c = 5 d = 2 Question 7 a = 25	Question 13 a = 0 b = 10 c = 0 d = 5	Question 19 a = 5 b = 15 c = 5 d = 5	Question 25 a = 8 b = 10 c = 15 d = 0

Your Entrepreneurial Profile:

225-275	Successful Entrepreneur
190-224	Entrepreneur
175-189	Latent Entrepreneur
160-174	Potential Entrepreneur
150-159	Borderline Entrepreneur
150-160	
Below 149	Hired Hand

Explanation of the Answers on the Entrepreneur's Quiz

Following is a discussion of the answers on the entrepreneur's quiz, as explained by Mancuso (1993).

1. It is only natural that a child who has grown up in a business environment is more likely to try his or her hand at the family business or a new business. Timmons (1999) has shown that this will occur more than two-thirds of the time.

2. This question is tricky; many would-be entrepreneurs choose to quit rather than be fired. However, the dynamics of the situation are often similar. The entrepreneur's uneasiness and compulsive need to be right could result in the termination of his or her job.

3. The need to succeed for successful entrepreneurs is often greater than for unsuccessful entrepreneurs.

4. An entrepreneur is at his or her best when he or she can control every aspect of his or her company.

5. The enterprising adult was usually an enterprising child.

6. The average age of successful entrepreneurs has been decreasing. In the 1960s it was around forty-five, while today it is in the thirties. However, this is not to say that a person in their fifties or sixties cannot be a successful entrepreneur. The field is full of

late bloomers. Take Colonel Sanders, for instance—he started in his sixties. He founded Kentucky Fried Chicken and did not stop there.

7.   The answer to this question seems always to be the same. According to Mancusco, entrepreneurs are commonly the oldest children in the family.

8.   Research suggests that the vast majority of entrepreneurs are married, and successful entrepreneurs have exceptionally supportive partners. A supportive mate provides the love and stability necessary to balance the insecurity and stress of the endeavor. A strained relationship will simply add pressure to an already strained business life. Bankers and venture capitalists look more favorably upon married entrepreneurs than upon those simply cohabitating.

9.   Education has always been a controversial issue. Some experts feel that entrepreneurs are in too much of a hurry to get an education. However, research has shown that the educational level usually achieved is a bachelor's degree, and the trend seems to be toward an MBA degree (Mancuso, 1992).

10.   Most entrepreneurs would rather work for themselves than answer to someone else.

11.   Past research indicated that a parent and child usually had a strained relationship. However, more recent research has disproved this theory. It suggests that because entrepreneurs are achieving higher levels of education and are not being forced to drop out of high school, as was the case in the 1940s and 1950s, they have better relationships with their parents.

12.   The entrepreneur works hard but probably doesn't even know it because he or she is enjoying the work so much.

13.   Entrepreneurs usually rely on outside management consultants and other entrepreneurs when it comes to making important decisions.

14.   Entrepreneurs are not high risk takers; they are merely calculated risk takers. They usually like 1:3 odds.

15.   Entrepreneurs need customers to do business, and bankers like businesses with customers.

16.   Many entrepreneurs have their businesses only as hobbies. These entrepreneurs are social and like to talk about themselves.

17.   Anything new excites entrepreneurs; they tend to get excited about new employees, products, suppliers, machines, methods, and financial plans.

18.   Usually, a person with a bright and low-key personality makes the best assistant. He or she is not likely to overshadow or butt heads with the entrepreneur.

19.   Organization is the key to success. This is the fundamental principle on which all entrepreneurial ventures are based.

20.   Along with organizational abilities, solving problems is what an entrepreneur does best.

21.   Entrepreneurs are participants, not observers. They are also optimistic. They believe that with the right amount of time and money they can do anything.

22.   Analyzing sales is the easiest way to measure success.

23.   Entrepreneurs separate business from personal decisions.

24.   Unless it is clear that one person is in charge, decisions are bound to suffer from a committee mentality.

25.   Entrepreneurship is a competitive game, and an entrepreneur must be prepared to

experience problems before experiencing success.

According to Martin (1999, p. 56), the ten ingredients for successful entrepreneurship are the following:

1. Plain, old-fashioned hard work and long hours.

2. Focus! You must be able to concentrate on what you do.

3. Look for good ideas, new ideas, new methods, and new ways to improve and grow.

4. Flexibility succeeds.

5. Adapt to change and learn to anticipate it.

6. Sell, sell, and sell! Entrepreneurs must be able to get others to buy into their idea.

7. Confidence! All successful people ooze confidence.

8. Balance between detail and general thinking. A sense of perspective is important.

9. All successful people use assertiveness to their advantage.

10. Constantly improve yourself and your company.

Key Terms

- **Business:** The buying and selling of goods and services in order to make a profit (Mariotti, 2000, p. 350).

- **Consumer:** A person or business that buys goods and services for its own needs, not for resale or for use in producing goods and services for resale (Mariotti, 2000, p. 351).

- **Franchise**: A business that markets a product or service developed by the franchiser, in the manner specified by the franchiser (Mariotti, 2000, p. 352).

- **Franchisee**: Owner of a franchise unit or units (Mariotti, 2000, p. 352).

- **Franchisor:** Person who develops a franchise or a company that sells franchises (Mariotti, 2000, p. 352).

- **Mentor:** A person who agrees to volunteer time and expertise and provide emotional support to help another person reach his or her goals (Mariotti, 2000, p. 354).

- **Partnership:** An association of two or more persons in a business enterprise (Mariotti, 2000, p. 354).

- **Percentage:** Literally, "a given part of every hundred" or "out of one hundred"; a number expressed as part of a whole, with the whole represented as 100 percent (Mariotti, 2000, p. 354).

- **Perseverance:** The ability to keep trying, even when the effort is difficult (Mariotti, 2000, p. 354).

- **Risk:** A chance of loss (Mariotti, 2000, p. 355).

- **Venture:** A business enterprise in which there is a danger of loss as well as a chance for profit (Mariotti, 2000, p. 356).

Chapter 5

Ethics and Social Responsibility: Internal Element

Learning Objectives:

- To discover how individuals develop their code of ethics

- To learn the consequences of unethical practices

- To learn why ethics are important in the workplace

- To discover how ethics and social responsibility apply to customers, employees, and investors

- To discover how issues of ethics and social responsibility affect small businesses

Generally speaking, a good way to decide if an action is within ethical bounds is considering the following statement: "If it smells rotten, it is rotten; stay away and do not swallow it." This is surely not an original statement, and it will not win any accolades as words of wisdom. However, it is this author's view of ethics, and it has proven worthy of remembering in many instances. I have learned that in the short run, unethical practices may seem like the best route; but in the long run, ethically and socially responsible practices will triumph. These are the thoughts of this author. But what do the researchers have to say about ethics?

Ebert and Griffin (2000, p. 80), state that:

> . In essence, ethical behavior is behavior that conforms to individual beliefs and social norms about what is right and good. Because ethics are based on both individual beliefs and social concepts, they vary from person to person, from situation to situation, and from culture to culture.

Ebert and Griffin (2000, p. 80) also suggest a deceptively simple three-step model for applying ethical judgments to situations that may arise in business:

1.   Gather the relevant factual information.

2.   Determine the most appropriate moral values.

3.   Make an ethical judgment based on the rightness or wrongness of the proposed activity or policy.

Today, there are many examples of ethical practices that reflect the concerns of the general public. For example, when Tylenol pain relievers were found to be laced with cyanide, Tylenol quickly recalled all the bottles and went public with the information. Enron provides an extreme example of the opposite sort of practices. The intensely unethical and greedy behavior of Enron's top managers was revealed thanks to the discovery of their corrupt accounting practices, which were laced with untruths and deceitful figures. Their corruption eventually drove the company into bankruptcy.

Many experts attribute Tylenol's response to the tampering scare to the company's ethical approach to running a business. The consequences could have been disastrous. Unethical behavior could have resulted in deaths, which would have led to loss of business, fines, and even imprisonment. Situations of this nature can fall under the umbrella of business ethics and social responsibility.

Social responsibility refers to an organization's response to social needs (Ebert & Griffin, 2000, p. 94). Only after the Depression of the 1930s and the social changes of the 1960s and 1970s were businesses forced to consider public welfare to some degree. Today, there is an increasing trend toward social consciousness, including a heightened sense of environmental activism and changing relationships with customers, employees, and investors.

Social responsibility toward the environment requires firms to minimize air, water, and land pollution. Social responsibility toward customers requires businesses to provide products of acceptable quality, to price products fairly, and to respect consumers' rights. Social responsibility toward employees requires firms to respect workers both as resources and as people who are more productive when their needs are meet. Social responsibility toward investors requires firms to manage their resources and represent their financial status honestly. There are general approaches to social responsibility that Ebert and Griffin (2000, p. 95) outline:

1.   Drafting a policy statement with the support of top management

2.   Developing a detailed plan

3.   Appointing a director to implement the plan

4.   Conducting social audits to monitor results

It is interesting to note that managers and employees of small businesses face many of the same ethical questions as their counterparts at larger firms. Small businesses face the same issues of social responsibility and the same need to decide on an approach to social responsibility. The differences are primarily differences of scale (Ebert & Griffin, 2000, p. 95).

Key Terms

- **Business ethics**: Ethical or unethical behaviors by a manager or employer of an organization (Ebert & Griffin, 2000, p. 80).

- **Check kiting**: The illegal practice of writing checks against money that has not yet been credited at the bank from which the checks are drawn (Ebert & Griffin, 2000, p. 90).

- **Collusion:** An illegal agreement between two or more companies to commit a wrongful act (Ebert & Griffin, 2000, p. 88).

- **Consumerism**: A form of social activism dedicated to protecting the rights of consumers in their dealings with businesses (Ebert & Griffin, 2000, p. 88).

- **Ethical behavior:** Behavior conforming to generally accepted social norms concerning beneficial and harmful actions (Eber**t & Griffin, 2000**, p. 80).

- **Ethics:** Beliefs about what is right and wrong or good and bad in actions that affect others (Ebert & Griffin, 2000, p. 80).

- **Social responsibility:** The attempt of a business to balance its commitments to groups and individuals in its environment, including customers, other businesses, employees, and investors (Ebert & Griffin, 2000, p. 83).

- **Whistleblower**: An employee who detects and tries to put an end to a company's unethical, illegal, or socially irresponsible actions by publicizing them (Ebert & Griffin, 2000, p. 89).

Chapter 6

Additional Elements for Survival and Success: Internal Element

Learning Objectives:

- To learn from the experiences of others

- To become aware of the unexpected

- To understand the importance of advance planning

- To understand the importance of threshold decision making

- To understand the importance of start-up finance and cash flow

- To learn to read the accountant's financial statements

- To gain insight into developing solutions for important management issues

- To gain marketing insights

Sooner or later, every businessperson will face an unexpected situation. Almost all business owners will confess that they are often surprised after entering the wonderful world of entrepreneurship because they did not expect to encounter a certain situation. Success does not come easy to any businessperson, and everyone faces challenges. Many face multiple setbacks; some fail miserably before succeeding. But each successful businessperson finds the will to press on and achieve a dream to reach a goal. This determination may be described as a drive to start a venture, scratch an itch, or realize a passion. However, before you do something you may regret, you should think about the information you need to launch the venture. If you do not have enough information or market research to point you in the right direction, now is the time to get it. If you lack the training and experience your particular venture requires, now is the time to get it.

Starting a business without the necessary knowledge is a recipe for failure.

The pre-start-up phase is the time of greatest impatience for any new business

owner (Norman, 1999, p. 1). You may be eager to get going—but first, be sure you are on

solid ground. After you are prepared, self-confident, and certain that your timing is right,

trust yourself to make it happen. The following are some important steps for starting a

venture and surviving the adversities.

1.   Prepare a Business Plan (Internal Element)

First and foremost, write a plan—a business plan. A formal, written business plan

is an invaluable roadmap for a new venture, so do not take it lightly. If you think the plan

is weak, study one more aspect of the business plan, analyze one more spreadsheet, look

at one more location, or redo what you have done until you feel you have done

everything possible. Only then should you get started. If you need help, consult with your

local Service Corps of Retired Executives (SCORE); its members will be more than

happy to lend a hand. See **Appendix 1** for an outline of business plans.

2.   Determine Your Organizational Structure (Internal Element)

How you structure your business is an important factor in its success. There are

important advantages and disadvantages for each type of organizational structure, so

consult with your accountant or attorney before deciding on one. Following is a list of the

various types of legal structure available:

- **Sole Proprietorship:** Simple and inexpensive to create and operate. You go into business either alone or with co-workers, but you are the only owner. The owner reports profit or loss on his or her personal tax return and is personally liable for business debts (Bygrave, 1997, p. 293).

- **General Partnership:** Simple and inexpensive to create and operate. Owners (partners) report their share of profit or loss on their personal tax returns. Owners (partners) are personally liable for business debts (Bygrave, 1997, p. 293).

- **Limited Partnership:** Limited partners have limited personal liability for business debts as long as they do not participate in managerial functions. General partners can raise cash without involving outside investors in the management of the business (Bygrave, 1997, p. 294).

- **Regular Corporation:** Owners have limited personal liability for business debts. Fringe benefits can be deducted as business expenses. Owners can split corporate profit among themselves and the corporation, paying a lower overall tax rate. This entity is more expensive to create than a partnership or sole proprietorship, and the paperwork can seem burdensome. A regular corporation is a separate entity with legal existence apart from its owners, the stockholders (Bygrave, 1997, p. 293).

- **S Corporation:** Owners have limited personal liability for business debts. Owners report their share of corporate profit or loss on their personal tax returns. Owners can use corporate loss to offset income from other sources. This type of corporation is more expensive to create than a partnership or sole proprietorship, and it requires more paperwork than a limited liability company, which offers similar advantages. Income must be allocated to owners according to their ownership interests. Fringe benefits are limited for owners who own more than 2 percent of shares (Bygrave, 1997, p. 293).

- **Professional Corporation:** Owners have no personal liability for the malpractice of other owners. This entity is more expensive to create than a partnership or sole proprietorship, and the paperwork can seem burdensome. All owners must belong to the same profession. (Bygrave, 1997, p. 294).

- **Nonprofit Corporation:** This type of corporation does not pay income taxes. Contributions to a charitable corporation are tax-deductible. Fringe benefits can be deducted as business expenses. Full tax advantages are available only to groups organized for charitable, scientific, educational, literary, or religious purposes. Property transferred to a nonprofit corporation stays there; if the corporation ends, the property must go to another nonprofit (Bygrave, 1997, p. 295).

- **Limited Liability Company (LLC):** Owners have limited personal liability for business debts even if they participate in management. Profit and loss can be allocated differently than ownership interests. IRS rules now allow LLCs to choose between being taxed as a partnership or a corporation. An LLC is more expensive to create than a partnership or sole proprietorship. State laws for creating LLCs may not reflect the latest federal tax changes (Bygrave, 1997, p. 284).

- **Professional Limited Liability Company:** This type of corporation has the same advantages as a regular LLC. It gives state-licensed professionals a way to enjoy the same advantages as a regular LLC. Members must all belong to the same profession (Bygrave, 1997, p. 294).

- **Limited Liability Partnership:** Owners (partners) are not personally liable for the malpractice of other partners. Owners report their share of profit or loss on their personal tax returns. Unlike an LLC or a professional LLC, owners (partners) are personally liable for many types of obligations owed to business creditors, lenders, and landlords (Bygrave, 1997, p. 294).

  See **Appendix 2** for the advantages and disadvantages of each legal structure.

3.   Line Up Your Cash and Credit Lines Before Starting Your Business: Internal Element

Many would-be business owners think they will get their money from banks and other financial institutions, but most new businesses finance their dreams through family, friends, distant relatives, and their cookie jars. Remember these tips when dealing with banks: good credit is important, start small, make friends with your banker, establish yourself, present yourself as a person worthy of a bank's confidence, and be prepared to personally guarantee a loan. However, you should know that it is illegal for a lender to ask your spouse to sign personally, so a bank should not even ask. In addition, you should try to chip away at the extent of personal guarantee the bank wants you to sign. Keep hammering and chipping away until you reach a level you are comfortable with. Your efforts in this regard will pay off.

4.   Start with What You Know (Internal Element)

It is always best to choose a business area you know and with which you have had some experience. However, this is not to say that you cannot enter a business area you are unfamiliar with—you just have to make sure you allow enough time in your contract to learn the ins and outs of the business. Spend time with the old owner to learn about the industry, market, operation, and, above all, the customers. Your learning curve will be shorter if you work in the business or a similar one before you buy or start the venture. If you have to, work for free.

5.   Do Not Buy Blindly (Internal Element)

Investigate the business you are buyin or thinking of starting, including the finances, lease (if you will be paying rent), customers, revenue, and cash flow. Remember that many established companies, like old houses, come with problems (Norman, 1999, p. 12). A company's location, for example, may be on the decline. Its reputation may be bad, or its equipment may be obsolete, broken, or completely depreciated. In addition, the seller may have an inflated view of the company's worth (Norman, 1999, p. 12).

As a prospective buyer, you should do the due diligence before jumping into the deal. First, talk to business neighbors to find out potential problems with location or the specific company. You can learn a great deal just by hanging around and observing the location and the business at different times during the day. A word of caution, however: be careful about telling anyone you are a prospective buyer. Word about a pending sale can harm a business and expose you to a lawsuit by the seller. (Norman, 1999, pp. 12, 23).

Hire a financial expert to examine the books of any company you are thinking of buying, and hire an attorney to review the sale contract. Consider hiring a business appraiser to determine if the business is really worth the price.

6. Make an Effort to Get the Right Location (Internal Element)

Location can be a make-or-break decision for many types of business. Although some businesses and organizations do not depend on location, most depend a great deal on getting the best location. For instance, retailers are dependent on customers, so they need a location with high visibility and adequate parking. Labor-intensive companies need to be near large labor pools. Manufacturers must be located close to highways, rail lines, or ports.

Business owners should evaluate their businesses before looking for a site. They must consider the following: their target market, who their customers are and where they are located, whether their customers need to find them, who their competitors are and where they are located, how much space they need, and whether their location accommodates the necessary signage. If you are not comfortable with your assessment of whether a location fulfills your core requirements, that location is not for you. Remember that other locations will pop up that will meet your requirements.

7.   Negotiate the Best Lease You Can Possibly Get (Internal Element)

You must search for and negotiate a lease with terms that you can live with and afford. If you do not own the property where your business is located, your lease will be a determining factor in your survival. It will not only be a make-or-break deal; it will also determine the resale value of your business. One word of caution: you should be fair-minded when negotiating a lease and aim for a win-win deal. You do not want to get the landlord so frustrated that he or she will take drastic actions to break the lease. For instance, this author once negotiated an unbelievable lease. However, this lease eventually frustrated the landlord so much that he blockaded the entrance of my business for one month. Eventually I had to close the doors and sue the landlord. I won the lawsuit, but I paid a lot of money to the attorneys and never collected a dime.

8.   Learn to Read Your Accountant's Financial Statements

Since it is vital to understand all the financial aspects of your business, you must learn to read and interpret the financial statements prepared by your accountant. These financial documents will likely be foreign and unreadable to you, especially if you do not have a mathematical background. An entry-level college accounting class will expand your understanding of what your accountant is trying to tell you. Financial information helps you, the business owner, develop a vision for your business.

Your accountant can tell you what is selling and the profit you are making on your products. Knowing this information is not enough; you need to translate the information into decisions regarding production, advertising, and the possible expansion of product lines and the business.

The bottom line on a financial statement is what concerns most small business owners. According to Vallario (2004, p. 107), increasing revenue is not the only way to get a better bottom line. For example, minimizing your expenses without increasing revenue will have a positive effect on the bottom line, as long as it is done within reason, without affecting the quality of the business's product or service.

Keeping your finger on the pulse of your business will contribute considerably to its growth and success. In general, entrepreneurs who see beyond their creativity and learn how to gather and read the barometers of growing a profitable business have an excellent chance of success.

9.   Think Marketing: Research, Target, and Sell (Internal Element)

Norman (1999) states, "Money is the most obvious business need, and marketing is the most overlooked" (p. 17). It is important to remember that in every business, revenues come from sales, and the genesis for sales is marketing. Marketing research, target marketing, market plan creation, and sales plan creation can lead to the much-sought-after goal of a sale.

Marketing begins with marketing research: knowing who wants what you are selling. It continues with targeting: figuring out who will be most likely to buy. It then moves on to planning: determining how a likely customer makes buying decisions (Norman, 1999). You can accomplish all this by creating a well-crafted marketing plan that combines the benefits of your products and services with the right distribution channels. The ultimate goal of all this, of course, is a sale.

10. Regulatory Roadblocks and Dead Ends (Internal Elements)

On the surface it seems that regulatory roadblocks and dead ends are external elements (elements over which businesses do not have control). However, a close examination will reveal that an entrepreneur really is able to control these issues. For instance, special licenses required by many states may make it difficult for you to enter certain fields without obtaining training, passing a test, or, in some cases, posting bonds. Some professions that require licenses are cosmetologist, mechanic, plumber, electrician, and contractor. In addition, some cities have environmental requirements, such as air and water pollution control. All of these may seem like impossible barriers to entry, but they are attainable and within your control. You must address these regulations and follow the protocol outlined by the governing authority.

Hendricks (2001) explains some common roadblocks and dead ends and what you can do about them:

- **Zoning laws and concerns:** You or your attorney should check zoning regulations when you open a new business, relocate, or expand your business. When you file an application at the local planning or zoning department, they will check to make sure your area is zoned for your intended purpose and that there are enough parking spaces to meet the codes. If you will want to locate to an area that is not zoned for your type of business, you can sometimes get a variance or conditional-use permit. To get a variance, you must present your case before your local planning commission. In many cases, you can get a variance as long as you can show that your business will not disrupt the character of the neighborhood where you plan to move.

Keep in mind that zoning laws can be hard to interpret. If you relocate or expand your business in a location that previously housed a similar business, however, you are unlikely to encounter any problems (Hendricks, 2001, p. 321). Thus, this is an internal element.

- **The OSHA regulation:** Created in 1970 to oversee workplace safety and health, OSHA has a litany of rules regarding everything from asbestos to workplace violence. Many business owners complain that complying with OSHA is burdensome; however, there is no doubt that the end result is a safer workplace, which is a worthwhile goal. There is also no doubt that complying with OSHA is required. The law dictates that if your state does not have its own workplace safety plan that is at least as strict at OSHA, then you must follow OSHA. You can learn more about your state's rules by contacting your state's labor department. About half the states have their own safety agencies and regulations.

- **Other regulations affecting growing companies that are internal elements:** Regulations can be a burden to small businesses. A study by Hopkins and Diversified reported that the regulatory cost per employee was highest for firms with one to four employees, weighing in at $31,748 per employee. For firms with more than five hundred employees, the regulatory burden was $16,241 per employee. Traditionally, regulations and the associated paperwork have been viewed as significant burdens for small-business owners (Henricks, 2001, p. 323). Henricks rationalizes that since the regulatory cost per employee is higher for small firms, one way to reduce the overall impact of regulations on your company is to grow your business. Becoming larger will reduce the percentage of resources you have to devote to keeping up with regulations and will allow you to grow still

larger (2001, p. 323).

Indications are that regulatory burdens will not decline sharply any time

soon. While there has been some effort to lighten the regulatory burden, the trend

seems to be an increase in another area when one area is reduced (Henricks, 2001,

p. 323).

11.   Debt Capitalization (Internal Element)

Businesses constantly need additional capitalization. Likewise, banks

and financial institutions are businesses and seek to grow and improve their profitability

as well. This can only be done if they find and bet on successful, young, growing

companies.

Like any business initiative, a loan transaction depends on the skills and resources

of those involved. A successful loan depends on a team of several players: accountant,

attorney, insurance agent, banker, and mentor. Your team should not be assembled solely

for the purpose of obtaining a loan. Rather, your business should have regular access to

the expertise of a banker, accountant, attorney, and insurance agent from the day the

business is started. The sooner you build your team, the more smoothly your business and

the loan process will proceed.

However, what every businessperson should know is that financial institutions are

what this author would call "fair-weather friends." Banks are notoriously fickle. They

loan money at rates lower than other lenders and cannot afford high losses without

getting into trouble with the Federal Reserve and FDIC. You face the risk that when you can least afford it, a bank may demand that your loan be paid off, thus forcing your company into bankruptcy (Fraley, 1998, p. 109). On the other hand, when you really do not need the funds—when things are going well—bankers are more than anxious to lend you money. When things get tough, the getting gets touch. The moral is this: get it while the getting is good. A businessperson may want to borrow for the future. Keep in mind that when reviewing a loan request, the loan officer's primary concern is whether or not the loan will be repaid. Many loan officers will order a copy of your business's credit report from a business credit reporting agency. For this reason, it is important that you work with the credit reporting agencies to help them present an accurate picture of your business. Usually the loan officer will consider the following issues:

- Have you invested savings or personal equity in your business totaling at least 25 to 50 percent?

- Do you have a sound record of credit worthiness as indicated by your credit report, work history, and letters of recommendation?

- Do you have sufficient experience and training to operate a business successfully?

- Does the business have sufficient cash flow to make monthly interest and principal payments on the loan?

You can consider several sources when looking for financing, and you should explore all your options before making your decision. Banks and credit unions are the most common sources for financing if you can show that your business is sound. Other sources of capital for most new businesses come from savings and other personal resources. Though entrepreneurs often use credit cards to finance business needs, there may be better options available, even for very small loans.

Know that the principal sources of borrowed capital for new and young businesses are trade credit, commercial banks, finance companies, factors, and leasing companies. Start-ups have more difficulty borrowing money than do existing businesses. Nevertheless, start-ups managed by an entrepreneur with a good track record, significant equity in the business, and a sound business plan can borrow money from one or more sources. If little equity or collateral exists, the start-up will not have much success with the banks. (See **Appendix 3** for a list of funding sources.) Ultimately, the most important aspect of successfully closing a deal is the person you deal with, rather than the amount, terms, or institution. In essence, a borrower is better off seeking the right banker than seeking the right bank.

Timmons provides several informative tables that are useful for businesses wishing to borrow money (1999, p. 493), including **Table 6**, Financing Sources for Business; **Table 7**, Debt Financing Sources by Term of Financing; and **Table 8**, Specific Lending criteria.

Table 6: Financing Sources for Business

Source: Timmons, J. A. (1999). *Financing and planning the new venture.* Acton, MA:

Brick House Publishing, p. 34.

Source	Start-Up Company	Existing Company
Trade credit	Yes	Yes
Commercial banks	Occasionally, with strong equity	Yes
Finance companies	Rare (if assets are okay)	Yes
Leasing companies	Difficult	Yes
Mutual savings banks	Rare	Real estate and other assets
Insurance companies	Rare	Yes

Table 7: Debt Financing Sources by Term of Financing

Source: Timmons, J. A. (1999). *Financing and planning the new venture*. Acton, MA: Brick House Publishing, p. 34.

Term of Financing

Source	Short	Medium	Long
Trade credit	Yes	Yes	Possible
Commercial banks	Most frequently	Yes	Rare
Factors	Most frequently	Rare	No
Leasing companies	No	Most frequently	Some
Mutual savings banks	No	No	Real estate
Insurance companies	Rare	Most frequently	Yes

Table 8: Specific Lending Criteria

Source: Timmons, J. A. (1999). *Financing and planning the new venture*. Acton, MA: Brick House Publishing, p. 33.

Security	Credit Capacity
Accounts receivable	70–80 percent of those less than ninety days
Inventory	40–60 percent depending on obsolescence risk
Equipment	70–80 percent of market value (less if specialized)
Chattel mortgage	100–150 percent or more of auction appraisal value
Conditional sales contract	60–70 percent or more of purchase price
Plant improvement loan	60–80 percent of appraised value or cost

According to David Newton, a professor of entrepreneurial finance and head of the entrepreneurship program at Westmont College in Santa Barbara, California, there are five basics that must be in place before you sit down with potential investors. If any of these items is not fully ready, your request will not fly. Investors will not give any credit for having four out of five of these items in the proper shape; instead, they will notice the one that is missing or not in good shape. Newton (2004) firmly states that the venture's portfolio of disclosure and readiness must be complete, with nothing missing across the board. The five important areas are the following:

1. Have a final, airtight version of your business plan.

2. Provide a personal financial statement of current income and past income cash flow for the past three to five years.

3. Make sure the management team is completely in place.

4. Get the supply-side and demand-side documents together.

5. Make sure your product or service is already being used by someone or by a company, at least in the beta-test form.

Only when these five elements are in place will an investor give you serious attention. Put yourself in the investor's shoes: would you invest in you? (Newton, 2004) You absolutely would not, if you were in financial crisis. What creditors want to see is that owners of financially troubled businesses see recovery as a process consisting of a plan to put the business back on a profitable track as well as a plan to pursue growth-oriented strategies.

A company in financial crisis will seek to return to profitability by cost reduction and cash flow increase. Therefore, one of the strategies in the plan for survival is to identify which assets are necessary and which assets can be used to replenish cash flow. An asset reduction strategy to improve cash can entail the following:

- Reducing inventory to maintain cash

- Negotiating for longer payment terms in paying for inventory and other payables

- Selling or leasing excess space, land, or buildings

- Eliminating aspects of the business that are not profitable

- Selling underutilized or surplus fixed assets

- Revising procedures to collect receivables faster

- Offering discounts for paying within terms

Obviously, cutting costs is important, and it can be accomplished by analyzing buying practices and identifying alternative sources of supply. This will entail informing your staff of what you are trying to accomplish and assuring them that their help and effort are valuable. Honesty with your employees will go a long way—you will need them to help you overcome your financial problems.

In short, an action plan for recovering from financial difficulties requires divesting yourself of surplus stock and converting it into cash. Analyze the level of stock you must have to conduct your business. Too much stock ties up your money, while too little stock loses sales and profits. Attempt to restructure your loan portfolio and your credit terms. Be aware that the worst time to look for money is when you need it the most. Release excess people, but retain your good people. You may have to be ruthless; if you are not, you could jeopardize the jobs of all your employees. Many businesses overpay invoices, so establish a procedure that guarantees that you pay for exactly what you get. Recalculate your payable invoices, making certain they are completely correct. Finally, watch every penny you spend and conserve resources, even to the extent of tying rubber bands together, using both sides of paper, and not throwing away files containing paper clips and rubber bands. This may sound crazy—but every little thing counts.

Key Terms

- **Asset:** Any item of value owned by a business. Cash, inventory, furniture, and machinery are examples of assets (Mariotti, 2000, p. 350).

- **Balance:** The difference between the credit and the debit side of a ledger; also the difference between the asset and liability sides of a financial statement (Mariotti, 2000, p. 350).

- **Cash flow:** Cash receipts less cash disbursements over a period of time. The cash balance in an accounting journal or ledger represents cash flow (Mariotti, 2000, p. 350).

- **Compound interest:** The money an investor earns on interest that was earned by the investment in a previous period, enabling the investment to grow exponentially (Mariotti, 2000, p. 351).

- **Creditor:** A person who extends credit or to whom money is owned (Mariotti, 2000, p. 351).

- **Equity:** Ownership in a company received in exchange for money invested in the company. In accounting terms, equity is equal to assets minus liabilities (Mariotti, 2000, p. 352).

- **Free-enterprise system:** An economic system in which businesses are privately owned and operate relatively free from government interference (Mariotti, 2000, p. 352).

- **Keystone:** To buy an item wholesale and sell it for twice the wholesale price; to double one's money (Mariotti, 2000, p. 353).

- **Leveraged:** Financed with debt, not equity (Mariotti, 2000, p. 353).

- **Promissory note:** A written promise to pay a certain sum of money on or before a specific date (Mariotti, 2000, p. 355).

- **Rate of return:** The return on an investment, expressed as a percentage of the amount invested (Mariotti, 2000, p. 355).

- **Return on investment:** The profit on an investment, expressed as a percentage of the investment (Mariotti, 2000, p. 355).

- **Risk:** The chance of loss (Mariotti, 2000, p. 355).

- **Venture capital:** Funds invested in a potentially profitable business enterprise despite the risk of loss (Mariotti, 2000, p. 356).

- **Venture capitalist:** An investor who provides venture capital for a business; he or she typically expects a high rate of return and equity in exchange for the capital investment (Mariotti, 2000, p. 350).

Chapter 7

Concluding Thoughts: Strategies for Success and Growth: Internal Element

Learning Objectives:

- Value and objectives of the Small Business Administration

- To experience total immersion

- To identify best practices for weathering a troubled economy

Small Business Administration

It would be remiss on this author's part to conclude this book without some mention of the benefits of the federally sponsored programs of the Small Business Administration.

The following information was obtained from the Small Business Administration's web site, which is:

http://smallbusiness.dnb.com/business-finance/business-loans-government/4019-1.html.

If you operate a small business and are in need of assistance, or a loan, you need to understand the services the Small Business Administration provides.

The Small Business Administration (SBA) was established in 1953 as an independent agency of the federal government. Incorporated within the Small Business Administration authority are other agencies, dedicated to offering assistance to and addressing the needs of American's Small Businesses.

The SBA is responsible for providing four primary areas of assistance to American small businesses:

1. **Advocacy**

2. **Management**

3. **Procurement**

4. **Financial Assistance**. Financial assistance is delivered primarily through the SBA's investment programs, business loan programs, disaster loan programs, and bonding for contractors. The SBA's business loan program is one of its significant areas of financial assistance.

The Mission Statement of the SBA is to "maintain and strengthen the nation's economy by aiding, counseling, assisting, and protecting the interests of small businesses and by helping families and businesses recover from national disasters."

The SBA Web site is an excellent resource for small businesses. It's very well-organized and easy to navigate and provides a wealth of information.

SBA Loan Programs

The SBA offers a variety of loan programs to assist small businesses. However, it is important to understand that the SBA is primarily a guarantor of loans made by private lenders and other institutions and not a lender itself.

Under this concept of guaranty lending, commercial lenders make and administer the loans, and the business applies to a lender, not the government, for the loan. The lender decides if it will make the loan itself or if the application has some weaknesses, which will require an SBA guaranty if the loan is to be made. A borrower must have been turned down for and be unable to obtain a traditional loan. The guaranty on the loan is available only to the lender, not the borrowing business. The guaranty assures the lender that if the borrower does not repay the obligation, the government will reimburse the lender up to the percentage of the SBA's guaranty. Nevertheless, the borrower remains obligated for the full amount due.

The SBA's business loan programs supplement the ability of certain lenders to provide both long- and short-term financing to small businesses that might not otherwise qualify for loans through traditional lending sources. The SBA may not guarantee a loan if a business can obtain funds on reasonable terms from a bank or other source. There are three basic types of SBA loan programs and several special-purpose categories of Section 7(a) loans, including:

- The Basic Section 7(a) Loan Guaranty Program

- The Section 504 Certified Development Company Program

- The Micro-Loan, a Section 7(m) loan program

The different sections under which SBA loans that may be obtained refer to sections of the Small Business Act. Below is a brief explanation of the SBA loan programs:

Types of Guaranteed Business Loans through banking institutions include:

- Loan Guarantee Program: The 7(a) Loan Guarantee Program is the primary business loan program, designed to help small entrepreneurs start or expand their businesses. The program makes capital available to small businesses through bank and non-bank lending institutions. This loan serves as the SBA's best flexible loan program for small businesses.

- 504 Fixed Asset Financing Program: The 504 Fixed Asset Financing Program is administered through non-profit Certified Development Companies throughout the country. This program provides funding for the purchase or construction of real estate and/or the purchase of business equipment/machinery. Of the total project costs, a lender must provide 50% of the financing, a Certified Development Company provides up to 40% of the financing through a 100% SBA-guaranteed debenture, and the applicant provides approximately 10% of the financing. Aggressive vetting of any property purchased through this program is required. Specific SBA Phase I Environmental studies are required. Guidelines apply as all properties are treated as "high risk."

- Micro-Loan Program: Available for up to $35,000 through non-profit, micro loan intermediaries, to small businesses considered not to be a good loan prospect in the traditional banking industry.

- Economic Development Program: SBA partners such as SCORE and the Small Business Development Centers (SBDCs), operating in each state, provide free and confidential counseling and low-cost training to small businesses.

- 8(a) Business Development Program: Assists in the development of small businesses owned and operated by individuals who are socially and economically disadvantaged.

The above information was obtained from the following web site:**http://en.wikipedia.org/wiki/Small_Business_Administration#Organizational_st ructure.**Once an SBA loan is approved, the SBA mails closing documents to the applicant for signature. Disbursements include an initial unsecured amount of $14,000, and subsequent disbursements depending upon construction progress and continued insurance coverage. After final disbursement, the loan is transferred to one of the SBA's servicing offices for management, or to its collections office in the case of default.

If a business defaults on the loan and the business is closed, the SBA will pursue the business owner to liquidate all personal assets. The IRS will withhold any tax refund expected by the former business owner and apply the amount toward the loan balance.

Personal Guarantee

Needless to mention a personal guarantee may sound simple and innocent, as well as harmless. Not so, think about it, all your life's hard work and wealth accumulation is at steak and such an action need to be considered seriously, and should be in consultation with an attorney and an accountant. Do not take such a step lightly, get prepared and seed the advice of professionals, before taking such a step.

A business owner may not think twice about signing a personal guarantee for your business. After all, you probably believe that your business will not fail. However, many financial experts would urge you to personally guarantee a business loan only as a last resort. If your business goes belly up, you stand to lose major personal assets, including your house, other businesses you may own, other real estate you may have an interest in, stocks, saving and checking accounts and any other assets, the creditors can get their hands on and turn it into cash.

Also, before you decide to personally guarantee a small business loan, think about what a personal guarantee means. Besides your personal assets, the guarantee applies only to you, if you are a signer of the personal guarantee, not to your business partners not to your managers, strictly to the people signing the personal guarantees. It means that you are declaring an individual pledge to make good on the loan, usually without exception. Depending on how your contract is written, you may be responsible for the loan even if your business is protected by limited liability laws as well as laws related to your corporate structure. Many lenders require borrowers to personally guarantee a loan or secure it with personal assets if your business is organized as a limited liability entity, or a corporate structure.

You may even be responsible for the loan after your business has been dissolved. When you issue a personal guarantee, you are acting as a cosigner on the loan. As such, creditors will go after you in the event that the borrower, your business, fails to make the loan payments.

Every loan carries some degree of risk, even if you do not personally guarantee it. In some cases, a lender may have the right to sue you personally if your business is a sole proprietorship or general partnership. It is important that you review section of this book on Corporate Structures, **(see Appendix 2).** If the lender successfully sues you, they can confiscate your personal assets to satisfy the loan. Another thing to consider is that if you are married, your spouse may have to cosign the promissory note. In that event, your jointly owned possessions are on the line for the debt, as well as your spouse's assets and income.

A word of advice concerning your spouse's assets and income, it is very important that you avoid your spouse from signing any personal guarantees for your business loan. In a "common law" property state, debts incurred by one spouse are that spouse's debts alone, and income earned by one spouse does not automatically become jointly owned. In a community property state, debts incurred by one spouses for a business are affected by both spouses. The community property states are: Arizona, California, Idaho, Louisiana, Nevada, New Mexico, Texas, Washington, and Wisconsin. (In Alaska, spouses can sign an agreement making their assets community property, but few people choose to do this.)

However, if you volunteer your spouses guarantee and use it as your bargaining chip; they will absolutely jump on it. It is not a good idea; please try to stay away from such a guarantee. In addition, if you are required to present your personal net worth statement, have only your name on it and divide you assets in half, if all your assets are in joint name. If you put both names on the net worth statement, the lender will argue that you both personally guaranteed the loan. Again, you must consult with your attorney and accountant on ways to make your estate as legally judgment proof as possible.

If you have exhausted all your other financing options, a personal guarantee may be your last resort. If that is the case try to chip away at the personal guarantee, by stating that the assets of the business are sufficient to eliminate the personal guarantee, or that you would limit it to a certain percentage of the personal assets. Guaranteeing a loan for your business demonstrates a high level of personal commitment to your business, which lenders like to see. Keep in mind that if you personally guarantee a loan to a business, you can expect a phone call from the lender if things go bad. However, it is important to heed the above advice concerning personal guarantees as much as possible.

In some cases, however, you may not have a choice if you want that loan. The Small Business Administration (SBA) requires that all loans they guarantee must also be personally guaranteed by any person with a 20 percent or larger ownership interest in the business. In addition the loans will typically be collateralized with some or all of the business's assets and possibly with personal assets such as a second home mortgage. If you are seeking an SBA-backed loan, chances are not likely that you could find much better loan terms through banks and other lenders.

It is almost axiomatic that entrepreneurs believe they can control their own fates. A review of this research journal will reveal that, except in certain circumstances, the majority of elements dictating their businesses' futures are internal elements, which means that entrepreneurs have control and can be the masters of their own fates. According to Timmons (1990, p. 114), this belief is one of the characteristics of an entrepreneur, along with learning from failure, persistent problem solving, and goal orientation.

As previously mentioned, entrepreneurs believe they can influence their own fates, and this strong belief is enhanced by their vision of the future. This vision pulls the entrepreneur through the daily details and problems he or she must deal with to get to the future. The ultimate goal of the venture becomes as real as or more real to the entrepreneur than life itself. Several visions of the future may exist in the entrepreneur's mind. These visions may shift and change as daily life eliminates, confirms, or strengthens them. When present-day problems occur, the entrepreneur may turn to the vision to identify possible solutions or to glean confidence in his or her decision making.

A corollary concept to future vision is total immersion. Entrepreneurs will immerse themselves totally in their endeavor: its operation, product, marketplace, venture environment, competition, current literature, innovation, and, of course, marketing, sales, and customer base.

Total immersion works; by applying enough intelligent hours, an entrepreneur cannot help but feel the rapture of the present-day situation when making intelligent decisions. Large companies do not deal in total immersion because it requires too much work and time on the part of paid employees. In place of this, large companies use more people to attack a particular problem. However, adding more people to the process of decision and action often means that there are more factors involved, more complications, more time required to move, more reasons not to move, more chances for things to fall through the cracks, and, ultimately, higher overhead and prices (Timmons, 1990, p. 116).

Timmons also comments that total immersion must last long enough in a new venture to get the company going and establish a solid market position. Once it is established, total immersion is not as crucial, but many ventures continue to operate this way (Timmons, 1990, p. 116).

Total immersion is not the only element required for growth and success. To develop into aggressive, growing, successful businesses, most new ventures need good rapport with customers, suppliers, bankers, consulting professionals, and other business stakeholders. In short, it is necessary to create the image of a winner, which builds a bandwagon effect that adds momentum to the new venture. Businesses want the tangible benefits of doing business with a growing new venture, and they enjoy associating with success early enough to prove they have the ability to discern it. This requires that they jump on the bandwagon, which means they supply the new venture with scarce materials, loan the venture money, and buy the venture's products. Success breeds success, and everyone wants to be associated with a successful business. As such, it is important for small businesses to maintain a successful posture, even in hard times. To be a success, it is important for businesses to know how to weather the storm of economic turbulence.

There are solid practices that small businesses should employ to help them succeed even in a bad economy. Following are some of these practices, not necessarily in order of importance.

Cash flow: Focus on cash flow rather that paper profits. This may seem like a simple practice, but in actuality, it is not. Cash is king in business, and no company can survive for very long if it is not experiencing a positive cash flow. A positive cash flow means that after paying bills and expenses, a positive balance remains in the checking account. It is important to remember that a profitable company does not necessarily have a positive cash flow, and a company with a positive cash flow may not necessarily be profitable. Cash flow is one of the most commonly used terms in business, which is why entrepreneurs must understand its importance and its real meaning. In hard times, cash flow is the determining factor for survival. If sales fall below the point where the company is able to produce a profit, panic may not be warranted as long as the company still has a strong and stable cash flow. A company can absolutely stay in business if it shows an operating loss but still maintains a positive cash flow. This can be accomplished in many different ways: using a reserve account to augment the cash flow situation, cutting back on inventory, changing credit terms by securing vendors' approval to pay a week or two later, or collecting receivables faster. Crack down on slow payers, and get rid of poor payers and troublesome customers. If you build a core of solid customers you can depend on, customers outside the core can come or go without jeopardizing your company's existence. Charge late fees to customers who fail to pay within your terms, and monitor customers who inappropriately use payment discounts. Your company's survival depends on ruthlessness and tirelessness in collecting receivables and maintaining a positive cash flow.

Gain lenders' confidence: Experience has shown that bankers and lenders are fair-weather friends. They throw money at your feet when you do not need it and hang you out to dry when you do need it. Banks do not like surprises, so it is important to let them know your financial position before they determine it themselves. Try to win their confidence and work with them in a partnering rather than adversarial way to make sure they will be there for you when you need them. This can be accomplished by meeting their covenants and sending them financial statements upon request in a timely fashion.

Know your break-even point: A company's break-even point is the point at which a product or service stops costing money to produce and sell and starts generating a profit. It determines what sales volume is required to recover the variable and fixed costs of producing your product or providing your service. In distressed economic times, a business must know its break-even point; it is, in a sense, the lowest possible level of sales required for making a profit. If the break-even level is tough to reach, a business must determine its burn rate.

Know your burn rate: In distressed times, the burn rate is an important feature for mature companies who are struggling or who are burdened with large amounts of debt. If companies burn cash too fast, they risk going out of business. Burn-rate analysis can tell owners and other stakeholders whether a company needs additional financing. The burn rate assumes that sales have dropped through the floor and that a company is facing a worst-case scenario.

Sell underutilized assets not producing a return on investment: An inventory of your assets and their usefulness can produce additional revenue to help your cash flow. If you have assets like old trucks or equipment, sell them off and add the revenue to your cash flow, increasing its positive level.

Borrow from the company's cash-value life insurance policies: Though pursuing this route can absolutely help your cash flow, it is the most overlooked technique available. Simply stated, if your company has a life insurance policy that earns cash value (not a term life policy), you can borrow from the cash value and not repay it until your situation improves. Best of all, you do not have to qualify. For companies concerned that they may not qualify for a loan, this strategy is heaven-sent and can help solve cash flow problems. However, it should be understood that the funds borrowed are deducted from the payout from the insurance company, upon the death of the policy holder, to the beneficiary.

Shareholders' loans to the company: Accepting loans from shareholders is another way to help your cash flow problem. It will show lenders that you are putting your money at stake and risking your assets.

Utilize credit cards for gaining additional cash flow: This may sound controversial and contrary to what credit analysts preach or teach, but I think it is an out-of-the-box tactic and well worth considering. Some credit card companies offer a business-class card—for instance, American Express calls theirs the American Express Corporate Card Program. It allows businesses to use the corporate account payable (AP) card to pay their suppliers. This provides you with an extra thirty days of cash flow, with no fees on your part. This particular program is unsecured, with a thirty to sixty-day interest-free line of credit for the business and no personal guarantees on the part of the owners, just an organizational guarantee. You may want to explore this option with credit card companies.

1. **Focus your time and efforts on high-return chores**: Studies have shown that executives spend half their time doing things other people should be doing and do not focus on building their cash flow. Owners should make sure they spend their time doing high-return activities instead of activities that should be done by others, such as sorting the mail.

2. **Utilize zero-based budgeting (ZBB) and analyze the variances**: ZBB is a method of budgeting in which expenses must be justified for each new period. It is timely now to talk about ZBB because we are now in the midst of a new recession and the effects are being felt through line-budget items. This budgeting approach involves comparing what you spent last year on expenses and what you

are allocating this year. In times of distress, these line items must be reviewed, and many may be eliminated, making it a zero-line item.

3. **Do not fail to communicate**: In many cases, a cash flow problem can be helped by communicating the situation to high-level executives, conducting open discussions, and brainstorming ways of improving cash flow. For example, eliminating unnecessary practices or customs can help improve cash flow.

You can change your situation and improve your distressed position by taking the necessary actions. The point I am trying to emphasize is that whether you sell your business, pass it on to a descendent, close it, or expand it, one thing is certain: life will go on. What happens to you depends entirely on you, whether you are in business or involved in another pursuit. It is true whether the company you started is still growing or, like an adult child, has grown up and moved on. It is still up to you.

Maintaining a positive cash flow is difficult during a depressed economy. However, it can be done, and your business can survive. A small-business owner must be diligent, observant, honest, willing to make changes, and willing to devote time and effort to keep his or her business going. Think positively and creatively, and seek experts' advice. One last bit of advice: try not to venture into the unknown during stressful economic conditions. Stick to what you know and what you are good at: your business.

Appendix 1

Outline of a Business Plan

I.   Cover Sheet

II.   Statement of Purpose

III. Table of Contents

A. The Business

    a. Description of the Business Idea

    b. Legal Structure of the Business

    c. History of the Company

    d. Composition of the Management Team

    e. Marketing Strategies

    f. Competition

    g. Operating Procedures

    h. Personnel and Staffing Teams

    i. Business Insurance

    j. Financial Data

B. Marketing

    a. Marketing Plan

        1. Products to be marketed

        2. Uniqueness of product

        3. Market niche (if any)

        4. Target market

C. Financial

  a. Loan Applications

  b. Capital Equipment and Supply List

  c. Projected Balance Sheet

  d. Break-Even Analysis

  e. Income Projections (Profit and Loss Statements)

  f. Three-Year Financial Summary

  g. First-Year Monthly Financial Specs

  h. First-Year Quarterly Financial Specs

  i. Cash-Flow Analysis

D. Management

E. Supporting Documents

  a. Tax Returns

  b. Personal Financial Statements

  c. Copies of Contracts

  d. Copies of Leases

  e. Copies of Licenses and Legal Documents

  f. Résumés of Principals

F. Remaining Pertinent Information and Plans

Appendix 2
Advantages and Disadvantages of Legal Structures
LEGAL STRUCTURES OF BUSINESSES

A business can choose to adopt a legal structure that best fits the owner's goals and desires. Below are the common legal structures a business may elect to adopt, along with the advantages and disadvantages of each. Adams (2000, pp. 334–337) lists the different legal structures businesses may elect to form. However, the table has been constructed for simplicity in presentation by the author

SOLE PROPRIETOR	PARTNERSHIP	C CORPORATION	SUB-CHAPTER S	LIMITED LIABILITY COMPANY
This is the basic form of doing business. You keep all the profits and are responsible for losses. Best for start-up phases and simplicity.	Created by agreement, it can be oral but should be in writing. The limited liability company is making this obsolete.	In this form you create an entity that is separate and distinct from you as an individual. The business reports taxes though separate returns, not through stockholders' returns. Forms must be filled out, and it is rather complicated and expensive. However, it offers many benefits.	Combines corporate liability protection with the tax aspects of a partnership. This is a popular structure, but there are restrictions. It is as complicated as a C Corporation.	This is a relatively new business structure and is currently permitted in thirty-five states. The tax liability is the same as a partnership, but it is limited to the assets of the LLC.
Advantages	**Advantages**	**Advantages**	**Advantages**	**Advantages**
Ease of formation, sole ownership of profits, control by one person, flexibility, and freedom from government and taxation. Owner reports profit or loss on his or her personal return.	Ease of formation, direct rewards, growth, flexibility, government freedom, and no double taxation. Owner reports profit or loss on his or her personal return.	Limited liability, ownership is transferable, separate legal existence. Stability, ease in securing capital. Draws on ability of others. Fringe benefits can be deducted as business expenses. Owners can split profit among owners and corporation paying overall tax rate.	Same as regular corporation except taxes on profits are extended to the shareholders' personal incomes. Limited double taxation. Liability is beyond the assets of the company. Owners report their profit or loss on their personal tax returns.	LLC is the same as that of a partnership. Liability is limited to the assets of the LLC. It has the limited liability of a corporation with the flexibility and tax status of a partnership. IRS rules now allow an LLC to choose between being taxed as a partnership or a corporation.
Disadvantages	**Disadvantages**	**Disadvantages**	**Disadvantages**	**Disadvantages**
Unlimited liability, unstable if owner dies, less available capital, difficulty in obtaining finances.	Unlimited liability, unstable, difficulty in obtaining capital, bound by acts of partner or agent.	Limited by laws, extensive government regulation, expense in forming, double taxation. Owners (partners) personally liable for business debts.	Taxed the same as a partnership. More paperwork than for an LLC, which offers similar advantages.	Complicated to set up and causes confusion. State laws for creating LLCs may not reflect the latest federal tax changes.

Appendix 3

Funding Sources

Source: Debelak, 2001, pp. 312–315.

Individual Sources:

1. **Self-funding:** This is money out of your pocket, either from savings, credit cards, or personal loans or from the sale of personal property, homes, or stocks.

2. **Family and friends:** This is one of the tried-and-true sources of seed capital. However, try to take investments that represent less than 10 percent of a friend or relative's total investment money. More than 10 percent will mean the friend or family member will have a large voice in the business. Be sure to have a written agreement that spells out the terms and repayment schedule, if any. The more the details are spelled out, the fewer problems there will be.

3. **Industry insiders:** These are the best people to tap for investments. They know the market, and they can even help you sell or make the product.

4. **Angel investors:** Angels can be anyone: your dentist, your neighbor, people at church, local philanthropists, or retirees. They are nonprofessional investors who invest in your company to help you get started. They usually will not know much about your business and rarely want any involvement.

Professional Sources:

1. **Professional investors:** These are investors who can put $50,000 to $1 million into a project. They are more like venture capitalists than angel investors. They usually evaluate your product and market carefully and negotiate a deal that is good for them. Attending Small Business Development Center conferences is a good way to find this type of investor.

2. **Venture capitalists:** These investors like to invest in companies with high growth potential, experienced management, and a sound business plan. They do not like to make investments under $1 million and want to know that there is a sales history. To find venture capitalists, visit larger libraries, which should have *Pratt's Guide to Venture Capital Sources* (published by Venture Economics).

3. **Private placements:** In this method of raising money from investors, you hire a broker to sell stock. It is similar to a public offering except that the stock from a private placement is not listed on an exchange where it can be readily traded. Investors are hoping the company eventually goes public.

4. **Initial public offering (IPO):** An IPO refers to the selling of public stock that can be freely traded. The advantage is that it allows you to sell to anyone, not just accredited investors.

5. **Community funding:** Some communities offer low or no-interest loans from the city or county, tax increment financing, or outright grants. You can access this source if you start your business in an area that offers these options; however, due diligence is necessary before making a final decision.

6. **Small Corporation Offering Registration (SCOR):** SCOR is a Securities and Exchange Commission (SEC) program that allows you to raise up to $1 million with much less paperwork and much lower legal fees. The program also allows you to accept investors you do not know or who are not accredited. Contact your local Small Business Development Center or local entrepreneur club to find more information and locate attorneys who do SCOR registration.

Other Types of Funding:

1. **Factoring:** This is also called receivables financing. Factoring companies will buy your receivables from you for anywhere from 4 to 8 percent off their face value and receive the payment as customers pay their bills.

2. **Bank loans:** Banks give loans, but they are not typically a good source of financing for new companies because they want collateral for their loans—personal collateral if you do not have business collateral. However, few people know that it is unlawful for banks to ask your spouse to sign personally for your loan, so do not fall in this trap; and let them know it is unlawful for them to ask. Besides an installment loan, term loan, or asset-based loan, you may want to consider a revolving line of credit loan, which you can draw upon when cash flow is low and pay off when cash flow is high.

3. **SBA loans:** Small Business Administration (SBA) loans are similar to bank loans except that they are guaranteed by the government; therefore, banks are a little more flexible.

4. **Other little-known means of financing:**

a. **Cash deposits:** Many companies require customers to pay a down payment of anywhere from 25 to 50 percent on orders, especially for custom-made products. This funding can them help produce products that you have sold.

b. **Borrowing money from orders:** If you have a big order from a reputable company, you may be able to get a term loan from a bank. Private investors will also issue a short-term loan from a bank. Private inventors will also issue short-term loans for a big order, but they will charge you a sky-high interest rate, and they will typically have a clause in their agreement that turns over substantial company assets to them if you fail to pay.

About the Author

Dr. Anthony F. Ciuffo earned his Bachelor of Science degree in business with an emphasis in marketing at Empire State College. He earned his Master of Arts degree in economics and finance at the State University of New York and his Doctor of Philosophy degree in the arts and sciences with a concentration in business and an emphasis on entrepreneurship at the Union Institute & University.

Dr. Ciuffo's doctoral dissertation, *The Effect of Small Local Government's Policies on Business in Nassau County, New York*, is a template for bridging the gap between local governments and their business communities. Dr. Ciuffo is hopeful that this work will inspire downtown revitalization and economic development within small local communities.

In conjunction with his Ph.D. program, he developed the following research projects: Entrepreneurship and Business Development, Entrepreneurship: Starting Your Own Business, The Art of Developing a Business Plan, Strategic Management, Management Theory and Practice, Leadership, and Family Business Development.

In addition, Dr. Ciuffo has authored and conducted the following workshops: Entrepreneurship, Preparing a Business Plan, Financial Analysis (Quantitative Analysis), Mathematical Analysis Applied to Business, Case Studies in Quantitative Analysis Related to Business Administration, Investing in the Stock Market: A Quantitative Observation, Quantitative Analysis for Decision Making and Forecasting, and Quantitative Techniques Related to Strategic Management.

Dr. Ciuffo serves on the advisory committee of the Business Administration Department for Boricua College and sat on the Business Advisory Committee for U.S. Congresswoman Carolyn McCarthy (D-NY, 5th District). He also served as Special Assistant to the Mayor of New Hyde Park for Business Development.

As an entrepreneur, Dr. Ciuffo has launched numerous business enterprises and is involved in second and third-generation family businesses. Dr. Ciuffo also holds a U.S. patent for a sock-fastening device, which he is in the process of marketing. He has been an instructor and facilitator in the Business Administration Department at Boricua College, New York. He is currently an advisor for the Business Administration Department for Scholastic Development at Boricua College. Dr. Ciuffo has taught Entrepreneurship in the adult education programs for the Valley Stream School District in Long Island, New York, and he holds certification from the NACCE Teacher Training Program.

References

Ablin, Jack A. (2004). *Market outlook from Harrisdirect*. March 2004.
Harrisdirect@e-mail.harrisdirect.com

Adams, Bob (2000). *Small business start-up*. Massachusetts: Adams Media Corp.

Anderson, K. (2003). *Defining entrepreneurship*. Kansas City: Kauffman Center for
Entrepreneurial Leadership Clearinghouse on Entrepreneurship Education.

Association for Enterprise Opportunity (2002, January). Microenterprise Fact Sheet
For Media. *Association for Enterprise Opportunity* (Web site). Retrieved April
19, 2002, from http://www.microenterpriseworks.org/news/factsheet.htm

Bangs, D. H. & Pinson, L. (1999). *The real world entrepreneur field guide: Growing
your own business*. Chicago: Upstate Publishing Company.

Brill, B. (2000). Profiles in Microenterprise. *New Village Magazine, 2,* 43–55.

Burstiner, I. (1999). *The small business handbook*. New York: Simon & Schuster.

Bygrave, William D. (1997). *The portable MBA in entrepreneurship* (2nd ed.). New
York: John Wiley & Sons, Inc.

Calmes, Jere L. (2003). *How to start a business in New York City*. New York:
Entrepreneur Media Inc.

Cunningham, J. Barton & Lischeron, Joe. (1991). Defining entrepreneurship. *Journal of
Small Business Management*, 45–61.

Debelak, Don (2001). *Think big: Nine ways to make millions from your ideas*. Canada:
Entrepreneur Media Inc.

Dumas, C. (1999). Training For Microenterprise Creation: The Case of The Center for
Women and Enterprise. *International Journal of Economic Development, 1*(2).
Retrieved March 13, 2004, from http://www.spaef.com/IJED_PUB/index.html

Ebert, Ronald L. & Griffin, Ricky W. (2000). *Business essentials*. New Jersey: Prentice-
Hall, Inc.

Fasiska, Edward J. (1994). *Entrepreneurial quotient*. Libertyville: Wonderlic Personnel
Test.

Fraley, David L. (1998). *Financial decision making*. Oregon: The Oasis Press.

Henricks, Mark (2001). *Grow your business.* Irvine: Entrepreneur Press.

Kautz, Judith (1999). What is an Entrepreneur. *About.com.* Retrieved March 19, 2004, from http://entrepreneurs.about.com/ (c20021301)

Low, M. B., & MacMillan, I. C. (1988). Entrepreneurship: Past research and future challenges. *Journal of Management, 14*, 139–162.

Low, M. B. (2001). The adolescence of entrepreneurship research: Specification of purpose. *Entrepreneur Theory and Practice, 25*(4), 17–26.

Mador, M. (2000). Strategic decision making process research: Are entrepreneur and owner managed firms different? *Journal of Research in Marketing and Entrepreneurship, 2,* 215–234.

Mancuso, J. R. (1993). *How to start, finance, and manage your own small business.* New York: Simon & Schuster.

Maravilla, N. (2000). A Profile of America's Entrepreneurs. *PowerHomeBiz.com.* Retrieved March 19, 2004, from http://www.powerhomebiz.com/vol14/profile.htm   (c20020941)

Mariotti, Steve (2000). *The young entrepreneur guide to starting and running a business.* New York: Three Rivers Press.

Martin, C. I. (1999). *Starting your own business: A guide for entrepreneurs.* Los Altos: Crisp Publications.

McCelland, D. (1961). *The achieving society.* Princeton: Van Nostrand.

McConnell, Campbell R. & Brue, Stanley L. (2001). *Economics* (15th ed.). New York: McGraw-Hill, Inc.

Norman, J. (1999). *Starting your own business.* Chicago: Upstart Publishing Company.

Price, Courtney (1999). *101 answers to the most frequently asked questions from entrepreneurs.* New York: John Wiley & Sons, Inc.

Questa Media America, Inc. (2004). www.questia.com. http://www.questia.com/PMqst?action=getPage&docID=70502357&keywords=&

Richman, T. (1997, May). Creators of a New Economy. *Inc Magazine.* Retrieved March 16, 2004, from http://www.inc.com/magazine/19970515/1492.html/

Schell, Jim (1993). *The brass tacks entrepreneur.* New York: Henry Colt & Company.

Siegel, Joel & Shim, Jae K. (1991). *Keys to starting a small business*. New York: Barron.

Small Business Administration (2002, May 13). Frequently Asked Questions. *U.S. Small Business Administration* (Web site). Retrieved December 24, 2009 from http://app1.sba.gov/faqs/ and Retrieved December 26, 2009 from http://smallbusiness.dnb.com/business-finance/business-loans-government/4019-1.html.

Stolze, W. J. (1999). *Start-up* (5th ed.). New Jersey: Book-Mart Press.

Timmons, Jeffrey A. & Olin, Franklin W. (1999). *New venture creation: Entrepreneurship for the 21st century*. Boston: Irwin McGraw-Hill.

Vallario, Paul, Jr. (Spring, 2004). The bottom line. *Northeast Carwasher. 9*(2).

Merriam Websters Dictionary (11th ed.). July 2003.

Wilson, George W. (1982). *Inflation-Causes, consequences.* Indiana: Indiana University Press.